WORLD RELIGIONS

AF086234

WORLD RELIGIONS
AN INTRODUCTION

GANGA SOMANY

Edited by Malati Kanoria

Published by
Renu Kaul Verma
Vitasta Publishing Pvt Ltd
4348/4C, Ansari Road, Daryaganj
New Delhi - 110 002

 an imprint of Vitasta Publishing

ISBN: 978-81-19670-93-2
© Ganga Somany
First Edition 2025
MRP ₹395

All Rights Reserved.
No part of this publication may be reproduced, stored in a retrieval system, or transmitted in any form, or by any means–electronic, mechanical, photocopying, recording or otherwise–without the prior permission of the publisher.

Book Layout & Cover Design by Rohit Gautam
Pictures: Common Creative & World Religions by Ganga Somany
Printed by Chaman Enterprises, Delhi

CONTENTS

Dedication	vii
Acknowledgements	ix
Editor's Note	xi
Foreword	xiii
Hinduism	1
Buddhism	27
Jainism	43
Sikhism	61
Judaism	75
Christianity	89

Islam	107
Confucianism	123
Zoroastrianism	133
The Baha'i Faith	149

Dedicated to the memory of
my late husband
Shri Onkar Mal Somany,
who has always been
a source of inspiration
in my life.

◆◆◆◆◆◆

To my seven lovely grandchildren—
Siddhant, Nitya, Anushkaa, Naisha,
Arjun, Dia and Jai

And to all the beautiful children in this world

— Malati Kanoria

ACKNOWLEDGEMENTS

Professor P Lal
Professor N Vishvanathan
Mrs Zena Sorabjee
J L Mehta

Rabbi Albert Fieldlanders,
Westminster Synagogue, London

Alan Brown,
Religious Education Centre, London

National Museum, New Delhi for permitting reproduction of Indian Miniature Paintings on pages 48, 53, 56, 107, & 109

EDITOR'S NOTE

This book was written by my mother, Mrs Ganga Somany, over thirty-three years ago. Today, however, when children are confronted with huge academic syllabi, they often benefit from condensed versions of literary works. With packed curricula and limited time, shorter adaptations offer crucial access to foundational concepts. While not a replacement for the original text, condensed versions serve as stepping stones, igniting curiosity, and paving the way for a deeper exploration in the lifelong journey of learning. This was the primary reason why I decided to shorten my mother's rather long treatise on different religions of the world to represent it in a shorter, more concise format that would interest the school-going child of this millenium.

The divisiveness of religion stems from a complex interplay of historical, political, social, and ideological factors and it has increased alarmingly over the last thirty years, ever since the time my mother wrote this book.

I believe that learning the basics of all religions promotes tolerance, enriches understanding, fosters personal growth, and facilitates global cooperation, making it an essential aspect of education in today's world. This understanding helps in breaking stereotypes and prejudices, contributing to a more harmonious and inclusive society which, in turn, will promote humanity to work towards common goals such as environmental sustainability and social justice. This will surely benefit all nations and mankind. More than ever before, it is now essential to promote this harmony among the youth and in schools.

Malati Kanoria

FOREWORD

Deep, profound books, scholar's treatises, commentaries on religions are so numerous that people wonder: why is there another book on World Religions?

The idea began with my visit to some eminent schools in London. It was interesting to find that they were teaching the 'Religions of the world' to their students. It was not an examination subject. It was just to introduce the subject in a concise and pleasant manner to children, who would otherwise remain ignorant about the great religious movements and the fundamental and inspiring ideas and ideals of the human race.

With modern means of communication, the world is shrinking. Daily, we are in contact with people from distant parts of the world. We have business, political, and economical relations with them. We are rubbing shoulders with them, all the time.

To understand and develop a deeper perception and rapport with our fellow beings on this planet, it is essential to have an insight into the culture, festivals, rituals, and holy creeds of their religions. All this combines to form the character of an individual and makes him or her act and react in certain ways.

There is so much conflict, bitterness, and misunderstanding in the world. Even different ethnic groups of the same country are at loggerheads. We should train our children to have mutual tolerance and respect, and to realise that the goal of human life is the same for everyone. The paths to reach the peak may be different, but the starlit summit remains the same.

As Charles Caleb Colton, an English clergyman and writer, puts it aptly:

'Men will wrangle for religion, write for it,
fight for it, die for it; anything but live for it.'

In this book, I have briefly outlined ten major religions. I have tried to make it an attractive book which has been written in simple language, so that it appeals to people of all ages. My basic aim is to arouse the curiosity of readers about religion and if inclined, to interest them to delve further.

I have taken the advice of philosophers and authorities of different religions, and got their approval for the scripts.

I owe a great deal to two scholars—Prof N Vishvanathan and Prof P Lal who have contributed and have taken great pleasure and interest throughout the preparation of this book.

Ganga Somany

HINDUISM

ROOTS

Introduction

The pale orb of the sun rises gracefully on the horizon, out of the tranquil waters of the mighty river. A mystic hush hangs over the place, broken occasionally by the rippling of the water and the gentle movements of countless humans, who are half immersed and silhouetted against the golden-yellow glow of the early morning sun. Thousands and thousands of devotees are praying, chanting, and paying homage to the Supreme Being. This is the magical *Kumbh Mela* which is held once in twelve years. For the devout pilgrims, it is a blissful sanctuary and an experience of relief from the cares and burdens of everyday existence.

Every year, up on the mountains, along the steep paths, pilgrims in hundreds climb steadily, speaking different languages and dressed in colourful garments. Oblivious of the hardships and the discomforts, they converge towards their goals—Badrinath and Kedarnath.

At the confluence of the three seas, at the very southern tip of the land, thousands bathe in the multi-hued waters of the ocean and then worship at Kanya Kumari.

One finds long, never-ending rows of ardent worshippers, queuing up, and waiting patiently for the sacred moment when they will have a glimpse of Lord Balaji at Tirupati.

What is it that attracts these people irresistibly from all walks of life, from all corners of the country, from all castes and creeds to these places? What is the unique factor that promotes this unity in their diversity? The answer is Hinduism.

In his incarnation as Krishna, the Lord declares to Hindus: *"I am in every religion as the thread through a string of pearls. Wherever you see extraordinary holiness, and extraordinary power raising and purifying humanity, know that I am there."*

The Hindu religion is all things for all people, and different things for different people.

The Hindu religion is closely linked with the geographical divisions of India. In fact, Mother India is a reference to the figure of a female which is possible because of the actual triangular shape of the land of our country. The rivers, the mountains, the fertile plains, all are closely bound with the Hindu religion. The whole nature is a focus of the sacred life where different places have different temples at which worshippers and devotees try to discover the meaning of God.

The most ancient of all the living eastern religions, Hinduism was not founded by any prophet, and is not composed of the teachings of any group of prophets. According to the former philosopher, the President of India, Sri Sarvapalli Radhakrishnan, "Hinduism is more a culture than a creed."

Origins

How did it all begin? To understand this, we must go back thousands of years when man worshipped nature and made

Ritual Bathing in a Sacred River.

his peace with various gods. To know Hinduism, we must trace its history to the invasion of North India by the Aryans, who came here between 2000-1500 BCE. They found a highly organised and developed civilisation in Punjab and in the Indus Valley, now referred to as the 'Indus Valley Civilisation', Harappa, on the banks of River Ravi which was the prehistoric capital of Punjab. Mohenjo Daro in Sindh, was on the banks of River Sindh. Their culture was centred around the rivers, and the fertile plains. The ritual of bathing in the rivers was popular. They were the centre of existence for the ancient people, and were thought of as 'rivers of life' and, therefore, considered sacred.

The Aryans brought with them their language and culture and were a great influence on the existing religions and rituals, but they never forced their beliefs on the inhabitants. Being a martial race, they established themselves in northern India and pushed the existing inhabitants to the south of the Vindhya Mountains. It is not certain if the religion of the invaders was absorbed by the inhabitants and how it affected them. But there was definitely a fruitful interaction between the religion of the invaders and that of the pre-Aryan people of the Indus Valley.

Originally, the Aryans were nomads (perhaps coming from the Baltic regions) and used to make 'animal' sacrifices to the gods who represented the forces of nature. In India, they were overwhelmed with the bounty of nature and attracted by the fertile land. Before long, they had settled down in one place and began to till the soil.

The Aryans worshipped many gods. When their physical needs were more or less fulfilled, their thoughts turned to spiritual matters and they began to speculate on the reasons of existence.

They had a highly intelligent class of priests, who inspite of having little knowledge of writing, composed hymns which were sung during the sacrifices. They were excellent in faultlessly memorising the hymns that were composed by others. They codified religion and established successive stages of religious thoughts and worship. They performed ceremonies around the fire, while pouring grain and butter into the flames, and sang special hymns praising God. These ceremonies were accompanied by complicated rituals which were known only to the priests.

With the elaborate rites and ceremonies, the power of the priests increased over the people and it was impressed upon them that only through the expertise of the priests could the comman man come into touch with the cosmic powers.

Through sacrifices and ceremonies, they held out hope to the people of rewards after death, and material gains in this life.

The Caste System or Varna Ashram Dharma

This was probably the beginning of the caste system or the *Varna Ashram Dharma*. The caste system represents four main social divisions in Hinduism. It was thought impossible for one person to be an expert in teaching, ruling, farming, and fighting. So, it was easier for families to choose different occupations that they were suited to or for which they had an inclination. Caste was presumably occupational, not hereditary in its origin. These castes were:

Brahmins : The Priests
Kshatriyas : The ruling or warrior class
Vaishyas : The artisans or workers
Shudras : Who performed all menial tasks

In the beginning, caste gave security to the society and enabled people to know exactly what they were supposed to do. But the three upper classes, with their vested interests, did not want to lose their superior position. What was initially a flexible system, later became rigid: birth and not proficiency became the criterion.

Shoots

It is very difficult to describe the spread of Hinduism or to talk about it as 'growing'. According to the testimony of scholars, Hinduism was fairly widespread in the world. It is possible to surmise that the ancient Incas and Aztecs who were mainly sunworshippers, were familiar with the worship of the Vedic Gods. However, today, Hinduism is confined to the land of its origin perhaps because Hindus did not believe in proselytisation, or converting other people to the Hindu faith. There is no ceremony such as 'baptism'. The feeling is that to be a Hindu, you have to be born a Hindu.

However, since Hinduism in some form or the other is the religion of the majority of Indians, we usually find it wherever Indians have settled. They observe all the festivals and fasts; and priests from India travel all over the world to give discourses, and conduct marriage ceremonies.

Rath Yatra - Chariot procession of the Hare Krishna Movement in India.

Hinduism could not spread as a worldwide religion because it is an individualistic faith. But lately, an interest in the Hindu thought has been created in the West by the *Swamis* and *Gurus* through Transcendental Meditation and Yoga. These include physical disciplines that are directed towards self-control, and restraint of the senses.

Holy Books and Scriptures
The Vedas
The oldest and theoretically, the most sacred books of the Hindu scriptures are the four Vedas.
These Vedas were transmitted by word of mouth; they were not written. They were heard and experienced; that is why they are called *Shrutis* (meaning 'revealed').

The four Vedas are Rigveda, Samaveda, Yajurveda, and Atharvaveda.

All Vedic writings are divided into two; the *Karma Kanda* or department of works (ceremonial); and *Jñana Kanda*, department of knowledge. The hymns and prayers of the mantras come under the first. The Brahmanas, especially the Upanishads, come under the second division. All are alike, Shruti or Revelation.

The Samaveda, a collection of verses is chanted at sacrifices that are addressed to Soma, Agni, and Indra. The third of the four Vedas consists of *samans* or melodies of Rigvedic verses that were chanted during the Fire sacrifices. There are 1,549 hymns.

The Vedas teach us that the soul is divine, but it is held in the bondage of matter. Perfection is reached when this bond breaks, and the word used for it is *Mukti* which means freedom from the bonds of imperfection, and freedom from death and misery.

The Upanishads

Though the teachings of the Upanishads are a part of the Vedic heritage, they transformed the existing Hinduism. This spiritual insight was known as Upanishads (*upa* - near, *ni* - down, *shad* - sit) because those who received this knowledge sat at the feet of their teacher. There was an intimate student-teacher communion.

There are 108 Upanishads, all of which have been communicated and written prior to the birth of Christ. Of these, ten are the most important.

Adi Sankaracharya

He chose ten Upanishads to make his commentary and made them intelligible to a wider audience.

In the Upanishads, the sages have expressed their intuitive spiritual experiences, and say beautifully in simple words that 'All paths lead to the same goal, and all rivers flow into the mighty ocean'.

Satchidananda

The Upanishads probe the mysteries of existence. They seek to answer the vexatious and perplexing questions of life such as, 'whence are we born, where do we live, and whither do we go after death? Who is the cause? Time, nature, necessity, chance, or the elements? Or, who is called *Purusha,* the Supreme spirit?'

The central thought of the Upanishads is that 'There is infinite existence (*sat*), absolute truth (*chit*), and pure delight (*ananda*)'.

'Hiranyagarbha': The Vedic Concept of Creation.

Hence, Satchidanand is the leitmotif of Hinduism.

The Upanishads denounced external Vedic practices of sacrifices and rituals. They recognised only one God, who is defined as self-existent, ineffable, and omniscient.

The Bhagavad Gita

The Bhagavad Gita is a handbook of instructions on how human beings can actually practice the subtle principles of the Vedanta in the workaday world.

It exemplifies the truth that Religion is philosophy in action. Srimad Bhagavad Gita, the Song Celestial of the Lord, occurs in the Mahabharata.

The Gita is the most important philosophical work of Hinduism. It is a discourse between Lord Krishna and Arjuna and is set against the background of the Battle of Kurukshetra between the warring cousins, Kauravas and Pandavas.

The Bhagavad Gita or the Song Celestial does not represent any particular sect of Hinduism. Essentially, it is ethical and sheds light on how a man can achieve perfection, and how he should think and conduct himself. The story is related to the Pandava Arjuna who is reluctant to fight and kill his relatives, the Kauravas. Finally, he is persuaded by Sri Krishna that it is his duty as a warrior (Kshatriya) to fight for a righteous cause.

Lord Krishna explains to Arjuna that one should do one's duty in a spirit of detachment, without worrying about the result, and in his case, without the desire to win. It should be performed as a service to God's will and executed for His sake. 'You art the doer, I am the instrument!' The guiding principle of all action should be Dharma—the eternal law which guides a person to do his or her duty in accordance to their *Swa-Dharma* or duty to oneself. The pure act *(nishkama karma)* is its own reward. The end never justifies the means.

The 18 chapters of the Gita are divided into three sections of six chapters each which describe the three paths to achieve salvation (*moksha*):

Karma Yoga : The path of work which is practical
Jñana Yoga : The path of knowledge which is intellectual
Bhakti Yoga : The path of devotion which is emotional

According to Lord Krishna, a man should do his duty in complete detachment from the self. 'Though seeing, hearing, feeling, touching, and doing everything with the senses, he does not involve himself but thinks, "I do nothing at all".'

The religion of the Vedas and the laws of the Smritis are expressed and depicted through the noble and heroic deeds of great men. These are related through analogies, parables, and stories, so they appeal to the masses, who relate themselves with the heroes, and from their actions learn what is right and what is wrong. The two most famous and deeply loved epics are **The Ramayana** and **The Mahabharata.**

Smritis, are the Remembered Traditions. They are founded on the teachings of the Vedas. They are the codes of laws, injunctions, and prohibitions that are related to social ambience.

How many Gods do Hindus believe in?

The correct answer is '*One*'.

'Then who are these three and three hundred, and three and three thousand?' 'They are only the various powers or aspects of God.'

The Hindu Divine Trinity

Brahma: The Creator

There are hardly any temples dedicated to him and he is rarely worshipped. His consort is Sarasvati, who is the goddess of learning and knowledge.

Vishnu: The Preserver

He looks after the well-being of mankind. When injustice and unfairness become predominant, he incarnates on Earth to redress the imbalance. His consort is Lakshmi, the goddess of wealth and good fortune.

Shiva: The Destroyer

He is the destroyer of the phenomenal universe. Kali, Durga is his consort.

She is the 'mother' symbol and the source of energy.

When injustice and lawlessness abound in the universe, Lord Vishnu comes into the world in various forms and shapes or incarnations, to drive away dishonesty and evil, and reinstate righteousness and purity.

There are ten incarnations of Vishnu.

The Hindu ethos of religious life consists of four stages through which an individual must pass:

Brahmacharya: or celibate student life
Grihastha : or stage of the householder
Vanaprasta : or retirement from worldly life to that of renunciation of worldly matters.
Sannyasa : or the most rigorous and last stage, owning nothing and attached to nothing.

Holy Men: The Great Interpreters

Adi Sankaracharya, a spiritual and philosophic teacher, emphasised the importance of the Upanishads. 'He was able to harmonise the apparently contradictory statements of the Upanishads into a consistent system.' He stressed that we are deluded and controlled by our senses. The idea of each of us as a separate identity is regarded as an illusion or *'maya'*. The senses delude us into thinking that the world is real and we accept the unreal world as real. However, the truth is that there is only one being, the *'Brahman atman* reality', without which the unreal world would not exist.

The theory of Sankara is known as *Advaita* or non-dualism.

He is believed to have toured India thrice and during these tours, he established the four centres or *Maths* or *Pithas* in the four corners of the country: Sringeri in the South, Badrinatha in the North, Jagannath Puri in the East, and Dwaraka in the West. They are visited by worshippers from all over India and are instrumental in uniting the country.

Ramanuja, believed in loving devotion to a personal god (*bhakti*). Sankara's views were very difficult to be understood by the common people, for he had suggested that worship and devotion were of secondary importance. But how could simple people worship an impersonal God? The Bhakti movement was a reaction to the severity and control of yoga. He accepted the authority of the Vedas, and the Gita, but gave special stress to bhakti, which involves a loving tender rapport between God and the worshipper.

During the medieval period, singing of devotional hymns was popular in all parts of India. The Bhakti singers taught ecstatic devotion as the main and best means of salvation.

The general tone in the songs was of ecstasy and rapture of a loving relationship with God, and was expressed with touching simplicity.

Modern Developments

In the last two centuries, a new spirit has emerged. The chief feature of this new direction in Hinduism is a deep sense of social service with the object of improving society by removing many old taboos, concepts of rituals, and caste prejudices which are being challenged.

Hindu Revival

Ramakrishna Paramahansa (1834-86) was the main influence in bringing the teachings of Hinduism to the masses and to the world. He was a poor Bengali Brahman priest who lived in a temple on the outskirts of Calcutta.

Ramakrishna Paramahansa studied the faiths of different races such as Christianity, Islam, Zoroastrianism, and Hinduism and came to the conclusion that *'All religions are one. They are simply different ways of reaching the same goal which is union with God.'*

Ramakrishna's interpretation of the Vedanta philosophy became popular. A group of able and learned disciples gathered around him and spread his liberal message. He was a gentle, semi-educated ascetic, but he radiated an astonishing depth of knowledge, understanding, and learning. Such was his spiritual power that he charmed all who came in contact with him.

Swami Vivekananda

He went to the Parliament of Religions at Chicago in 1893

and electrified the audience by addressing them as 'Sisters and Brothers of America'. He spread the message of the Vedanta and directed the people onto the path of peace and serenity.

Vivekananda presented a new thought of one world, when he said, *'If one religion be true, then all others must be true. Thus, the Hindu faith is yours as much as mine.'*

He restored faith to the educated Hindus and taught them to absorb from the west all that was good and useful in science and technology. His clarion call to the nations of the world was that *'The Parliament of Religions has proved to the world that holiness, purity, and charity are not the exclusive possessions of any church in the world—upon the banner of every religion will soon be written, in spite of resistance:*
Help and not fight.
Assimilation and not destruction.
Harmony and Peace and not Dissension.'

Holy Places

Pilgrimage centres or Holy Places are an important feature of Hindu life. Millions of people across the length and breadth of India go to worship at these holy places whose origins are shrouded in a shadowy past. Some of these holy places are high up in the Himalayas.

Significance of Temples

The one cure for all human ills is the power to endure them with faith in the power of God's grace. Bhakti alone can give the power of endurance. Temples are places for the cultivation of Bhakti. What is the significance of making offerings to the images installed in temples? This is done as an expression of gratitude to the power that created all things. Only the best and choicest should be offered to God. Not everyone can do pooja at home, or make these offerings. The sight or the image or the Darsanam will itself elevate our minds and make us remember the source from which we came.

H H Kanchi Acharya

1) Lord Venkateshwara Temple, Hyderabad.
2) Pilgrims receiving blessings at the Lord Venkateshwara Temple.
3) Badrinath: A famous pilgrimage place for the Hindus.
4) Dwarka Temple in Gujarat, the abode of Lord Krishna.

The Symbols

The symbols in Hindu religion are of great significance. During rituals, they serve as channels of worship. The symbols represent a concrete expression of the religious experience of the devotee.

Thus, the mudra, a seal, or a mark (*tilak*) signify certain implications and ideas and become symbols of the Ultimate Truth. The symbols represent a mass of ideas and thoughts that are compressed in the form of some sign or the other.

Om

All mantras or prayers and auspicious communication begins with the sound of 'OM'. It is the most sacred sound. It is believed to be the first sound that reverberated in the universe. This sound includes all that has happened and all that is about to happen (*Mandukyopanishad*). It is a combination of three letters - A, U, and M.

The sound 'A' signifies Vishnu
The sound 'U' signifies Shiva
The sound 'M' signifies Brahma

Swastika

It is a symbol of auspiciousness. It has also been used as a symbol of the Sun or Lord Vishnu. It represents a changing world. This symbol is used on doors, buildings, and letterheads, to protect the believer from all evils, calamities, or from disasters of nature.

Coconut

The offering of a coconut on any auspicious occasion

symbolises the desire of the individual to realise the Supreme Truth. It is offered to the deities in temples; and at home, a devout Hindu householder makes it an integral part of his ritual while praying to God.

Flowers

The offering of flowers during worship symbolises the picking of desires and laying them before God. Vedic religion was not an idolatorous one. There were no temples, and people communed with the gods without the mediation of priests.

Law of Karma or Re-birth

The moral law of *Karma* is the expression of nature of the Absolute. Freedom and Karma are two aspects of the same reality. Karma implies resignation to the past, and hope for the future. Bad Karma can be destroyed and good Karma can be rebuilt. The concept of re-birth is a corollary to the law of Karma. The soul is not annihilated at death. Life eternal is the union with Brahman. The undelivered soul is subject to the law of births and deaths and has to work out its destiny by lives on Earth. The kind of birth depends on the nature of work.

Upanishads

'Karma changes, but the universal self, endures.'

Image Worship

The Hindu believes that he is a pure spirit. 'The sword cannot pierce the atman, the fire cannot burn it, water cannot melt it, the air cannot dry it.'-Gita

An ordinary mortal needs an external image to worship. It helps to keep his mind fixed on the Supreme Being to whom he prays. He knows that the image is not God, but it is His symbol. He associates the ideas of holiness, truth, and purity with different images and forms. In every temple, worshippers apply all attributes of God including omnipresence, to the images.

Parvati

She is known by many names such as Durga, Kali, Chandi, Uma. She is the goddess of the universe. She assumes different forms to suit the prayers or wishes of the worshipper.

Parvati is Shiva's spouse, and is known as the 'Great Mother', the kind and gentle one. In South India, she is worshipped in her fierce and terrible form, and her fury is unleashed on sinners and evil doers. In Bengal, Kali is worshipped in her awesome aspect, and also, by the Shakti cult. But even in her fearful form, she grants peace and ecstasy to her followers by conquering their fears.

Ganesha

He is the elephant-headed, pot-bellied god, who is a popular and lovable deity. He is portrayed with a single tusk, sitting on a mouse, and protects his devotees from all evils. Before starting any auspicious work or the daily routine of life, the Hindu first prays to Lord Ganesha or Vinayaka and invokes his blessings to remove all obstacles.

Hanuman

He is the son of the Wind God and is famous in the epic Ramayana. His form portrays dexterity and intelligence, and curiosity to gather knowledge. He is the perfect devotee of Sri Rama and helped him in rescuing Sita from Ravana. When the Hindus want to accomplish anything, they pray to Hanuman to intercede with Rama on their behalf.

Kartikeya

He is the God with six heads. He is depicted as riding a peacock and is worshipped as the granter of boons and intelligence.

Festivals

Hindus are very fond of festivals, and have a long list of celebrations. Festivals are usually linked with seasonal changes and reaping of harvests. Interestingly, the same festival is associated with different stories and events in different parts of India. India follows the lunar calendar, so the dates do not always coincide with the solar calendar. Some of the important festivals are Deepawali, Holi, Durga-Puja/Navratri, Onam, Pongal and Sankranti.

Worship

For Hindus, worship is not confined only to the temple. Most Hindus have a special corner in their house, or a separate room which they decorate with pictures of gods and goddesses and images of different deities. After a bath in the morning, they first recite their prayers and worship God, which is called *Puja*.

Usually, they repeat the name of God (Rama, Krishna or Shiva) on a *mala* or a string of 108 beads, or they may meditate or sing devotional songs. Arati (singing of hymns) is performed at the end of the Puja.

Activity Time
1) Think about a time when you did something good or bad. Did you feel happy or guilty afterwards?
2) Do you think Hinduism is just about going to a temple or praying, or is it about how we live our daily lives and treat others?
3) Imagine you have many friends, each with their own special qualities. That's kind of like the many gods and goddesses in Hinduism, each with their own powers and stories! What is your special power that differentiates you from others?
4) How does the idea of being reborn into a new body make you feel? Do you think this is possible? Who/what would you like to be reborn as?
5) The Bhagavad Gita is like a guidebook for life; it teaches us to do our best, be brave, and make good choices. Can you think of a time when you helped someone or were kind to someone? How did it make you feel?
6) Imagine a superhero who comes to save the world in different forms. That's kind of like the ten avatars of Lord Vishnu! Can you think of a favourite superhero who transforms himself to help in different ways?
7) How do you think Brahma, Vishnu, and Shiva work together like a team?
8) Do you have any daily routines or traditions that are important to you?

9) Bhakti is like having a strong feeling of love and devotion to God. It helps us feel closer to God and find happiness and peace. Have you ever felt really happy when you do something nice for someone you care about?
10) Adi Sankaracharya said that God is everywhere, like air we can't see but it is all around us. Ramanuja said that God is like a personal friend who is always there for you. Do you believe God is omnipresent?
11) Shruti is like a holy book with God's words, and Smriti is like a guidebook with wise advice. Which type of book do you like more: one with important messages or one with helpful tips?
12) Festivals play a very important part in Hindu religion. Describe two main Hindu festivals.
13) What do you find the most interesting in Hinduism?

BUDDHISM

ROOTS

Introduction

Once upon a time, a man was asked a direct question by some strangers:
'Are you a God?'
He replied, 'No.'
'An Angel?'
'No.'
'A Saint?'
'No.'
'Then what are you?'
And, the man answered: 'I am awake.'

This is the story of a man who was awake—Buddha, the Enlightened One.

Birth

Siddhartha Gautama, later known as Buddha, the founder of Buddhism, was born about 560 BCE in a village near the mountains called Lumbini, between India and Nepal, and attained *Mahaparinirvana* at the age of around eighty.

His father, Suddodhana, was the ruler of the small state of Kapilavastu, and his mother, Maya, was a beautiful lady of great virtue and purity. According to legend, one night, in her dream, Maya saw a white elephant holding a white lotus in his trunk, enter her womb. Ten months later, under auspicious signs and supernatural portents, a child was born to her. Maya was on the way to her parent's house when she delivered the child in a grove of sal trees. Seven days later, she died.

Youth

The young Prince Siddhartha (he who has reached his goal) was brought up in great luxury, by his mother's sister Mahapatriyapati. He was instructed in all the arts and sciences that a Prince should know, and was an excellent student. It had been prophesied that the boy would become either a great ruler or a mendicant. King Suddodhana was so apprehensive about this that he sheltered his son from the harsh realities of life, and resolved that he would never know the sorrows of the world.

Prince Siddhartha was married to a lovely girl called Yashodhara. He was surrounded by beautiful dancers, women, musicians, and showered with all the luxuries of life. Every sign of disease, misery, and death was removed from the king's palace and grounds, so that Siddhartha would not even know, let alone be exposed to these sorrows.

In time, Prince Siddhartha had a son, who he named 'Rahul', meaning 'obstacle', for inspite of his love for his son, he now felt chained to the world.

Suffocated by luxury, he sought something more fulfilling. One day, when the Prince went outside his palace, he happened to see strange disturbing sights.

Misgivings

He saw the sufferings and misery of the world in three forms, a frail old man, an invalid tortured by illness and pain, and a funeral procession with mourners. Siddhartha was ignorant of old age, sickness, and poverty, and had never imagined life ending in death. Amazed and troubled, he asked what all this meant.

He was told that this was the fate of all mankind and death came to all in the end. To be born was to die, and anyone who had taken birth, had to face illness and misery of old age. Deeply perplexed, he returned to his palace.

But, when next he encountered a monk with a peaceful and serene face, travelling around with nothing but a begging bowl, he realised that his life of pleasure and luxury was a mirage. He now longed for true knowledge and fulfilment of the self. He sought freedom to discover for himself what life was meant for, but he could not do that as long as he was in the palace. One night, he rose quickly and ordered Channa, his faithful servant, to saddle Kanthaka, his white horse.

Flight

The young Prince cast a last lingering look at his sleeping wife and son. He hesitated for one moment, but then he quietly closed the door and vaulted onto the back of his favourite horse, Kanthaka and rode away. Legend says that when Kanthaka left his master, he was so sad at the parting that he died soon after of a broken heart.

When far from the city, Siddhartha cast off his fine garments and put on a hermit's robe. He cut off his hair with his sword and sent them back to his father along with his royal garments. His hair curled to the right, the mark of a great man. He left a single strand of hair which was bound into a top knot and which is called *'ushnisha'*.

Ascetism

In the beginning, Siddhartha endeavoured in the traditional Hindu way by struggling through Yoga, and mortification of the flesh to realise his self. These exercises became increasingly severe and he subjected himself to extreme penance and self-denial, almost starving to death. There is a touching legend, very likely based on fact, that is connected with this part of Buddha's life. It is said that he had been reduced to skin and bones and was on the verge of death when a courtesan named Sujata, moved by his condition, offered him a bowl of *Kshira* (rice in sweetened boiled milk).

Buddha accepted this gratefully and remarked, 'Never in my life have I tasted such delicious food.' He realised that he still craved for good food, and fasting was not the way to salvation or Nirvana.

Siddhartha despaired of ever finding a way out. He felt that 'this is not the way to perfect knowledge nor to liberation. True meditation is produced in him whose mind is self-possessed and is at rest and fasting is not a solution. This step should be avoided along with other extremes of life devoted to pleasure and lust.' He sat under a Bo Tree and contemplated till he attained Enlightenment. He said, 'Never from this seat will I stir until I have attained the supreme and absolute wisdom.'

The Main Streams of Buddhism

GAUTAMA THE BUDDHA

THERAVADA
The strict 'doctrine of the elders'

MAHAYANA
The 'large vehicle', accommodating many different beliefs

Japanese sects — Shinto

Ch'an/Zen — Chinese meditative practice

Vajrayana/Lamaism/Tibetan Buddhism — Tantism, occult, Tibetan Bon

Attainment of Nirvana

Gautama Buddha sat for forty-nine days under the tree till he gained supreme experience of Nirvana and he became Buddha or the 'Free Soul'. It is said that Nirvana was arrived at in three stages. On the first night of meditation, he saw his previous lives pass before him. On the second night, he saw with a supernatural insight the cycle of birth, death, and rebirth and the relentless laws governing all life. On the third night, the four holy truths were revealed to him, the fact of suffering (*dukkha*), the source of suffering (*tanha*), the removal of suffering (*Nibbana*), and the way to the removal of suffering (*Dharma*).

Mara Tempts

While Buddha meditated under the Bo Tree, he was assailed by a tempter called Mara, who offered him all the physical delights and joys of the world. These were in the form of Mara's three ravishing daughters called Desire, Pleasure, and Passion. On Mara's demand that he abandon his quest for Nirvana, Buddha's reply was emphatic. He said, 'Why do you tempt me, O Mara? Do you not know that a Buddha who has made up his mind does not swerve from the path?'

Buddha Preaches

For some time, he was undecided whether to preach his revelations to the world, for he thought it would be difficult for the people to understand his message. However, he went to the Deer Park near Varanasi, where his first five former disciples had settled.

Here, he preached his first sermon, or as Buddhists say,

'set in motion the wheel of law.' The people hearing his words of hope and how to attain salvation, became his followers. His teachings were aimed at ordinary men and women who had no thoughts of entering monastic life. Later, he instructed his disciples to spread the truths of the Buddha Dharma in all four directions. In effect, they were a missionary order, and the sense of the universal mission that Buddha held, and which had no parallel in the prevailing religious history of India.

Buddha established an order of monks called *Bhikkus*. The Bhikkus wore the saffron robes of the Order, and followed certain disciplines which as per tradition were laid down by Buddha. There are many stories of the long years he spent in preaching his sermons. He returned to Kapilavastu, and converted his father, wife, and son Rahul to his faith.

He succeeded in transforming even his jealous cousin, Devadutta, who had plotted to kill him, by letting loose a mad elephant in his way. As the story goes, instead of harming him, the beast bowed before the great Master, acknowledging his supremacy.

It is said that once, walking between the assembled armies of the Sakyas and Kaliyas, he convinced their soldiers on the futility of war and bloodshed and thereby averted a war.

The End

For over forty years, his fame and popularity grew and the *Sangha* (the Buddhist order) flourished. Travelling with his disciples throughout the Ganges River basin, he devoted his life in proclaiming the liberating truth of dharma and nirvana. He had a long, calm, and peaceful life and he was venerated by all.

Preparing his disciples for his death, he journeyed

northwards to the home of his youth. Reaching the outskirts of Kusinagar town, he lay down and rested under a Sal Tree. That night, he passed away. He was eighty years old. His last words were, 'All things that consist of component parts will perish. Work out your salvation with diligence.' His disciples cremated his body with great sorrow.

Shoots

Buddhism has undergone many transformations since the death of its founder by appearing in different popular forms.

Buddhism ranges from basic simple piety of monks and nuns to the deep insights of Japanese Zen masters. It practises non-ritual simplicity to highly complicated Tantric practices as in Tibet.

Holy Books and Scriptures

The Dhammapada is the most significant of the *'Tripitaka'* or the 'Three Baskets', which represent the sum of Buddha's teachings.

'The Tripitaka' have been handed down to us in three languages—Pali, Sanskrit, and Chinese. These are:
Vinaya Pitaka
Abhidhanona Pitaka
Sutta Pitaka

The books have been written in Pali. These are the oldest and probably the most authentic records of the sayings and sermons of Buddha. These were memorised by monks and orally passed down over generations for several hundred years.

In the later period, the books were written in Sanskrit and Chinese.

Buddha lived at a time when a highly prosperous civilisation flourished in India. Rival ideas of religion continued to impress the minds of people. There were controversies and speculations. The philosophy of the Vedas and Upanishads were too abstract and idealistic to touch the lives of the common people. As a result, rituals, ceremonies, and superstitions prevailed.

Buddha's message was 'Go unto all lands and preach this gospel. Tell them that the poor and the lowly, the rich and the high are all one, and that all castes unite through this religion, as do the rivers in the sea.

'Not by birth but his conduct alone, does a man become low caste or a Brahmin.'

Buddha was a truly historic reformer who wanted to bring back the spirit of noble ethics and morality in the practice of everyday religion. He insisted that a spirit of enquiry and reason should be the basis of religious faith. He did not deny, refute, or repudiate existing beliefs, but he showed an alternative path to those who had the courage to think for themselves and follow the light of individual reasoning.

He accepted two basic tenets of Hindu doctrine, Karma and Reincarnation. Karma is the universal law of cause and effect which governs the physical, mental, and moral life of mankind. Good actions breed good results, and evil actions beget evil.

The other law which Hinduism believes in strongly, and Buddhism accepts as part of its philosophical outlook, is the Law of Reincarnation. According to this, all human beings reap the fruits of their good or evil actions 'on a collective basis', by having noble or lowly births.

The third tenet of Hinduism which Buddha endorses, though in a transformed manner, is of Moksha or liberation. As birth and re-birth are a kind of bondage, the aim of moral living and religious faith is to find release from that bondage. The abolition of Karmic reincarnation is the goal of Dharma. For Hindus, this is Moksha; for Buddhists, this is Nirvana.

Buddha did not depend on traditional texts to formulate his philosophy of life. His originality and greatness lies in the fact that he realised these basic truths through personal experience. The truths he attained have an intense and elementary simplicity. These are four noble truths in the following order:

(1) **Dukkha (suffering):** According to Buddha, universal suffering is an absolute fact. Such suffering can be physical, mental, or emotional. It may be the result of past karma, or it may be the result of deeds done in this life.

(2) **Tanha (craving or desire):** Ultimately, suffering is caused by human ego which hankers for material things because material possessions can never give true satisfaction. Desire is a fire that ignites more desire.

(3) **Nibbana (extinction):** This craving of the ego can be extinguished.

(4) **Dhamma (path of righteousness):** Extinction of hankering can be achieved if a human being determines to follow the path of Dhamma, which means the path of Reason and Goodness.

This is the path which leads to stability. Dharma signifies the Eight-Fold Path, which, if followed, pulls out desire and leads to Nirvana. For a householder, it is not always easy to lead a spiritual life, or renounce the world, but Buddha showed how to lead a happy life by following a moral path and doing good. The Eight-Fold Path consists of:
- Right Knowledge
- Right Attitude
- Right Speech
- Right Action
- Right Occupation
- Right Effort
- Right Mindfulness
- Right Concentration

In his own words, Buddha says, 'Entering on this path you will make an end of pain.'

Buddha also preached the five fundamental ethical principles or *Panch Shila*, which can be practised by lay people. This is: The Buddhist Credo:
Buddham Saranam Gacchami
Dhamman Saranam Gacchami
Sangam Saranam Gacchami

These words are recited by Buddhists in the form of an incantation. They mean:
I surrender to Buddha
I surrender to Dharma
I surrender to the Sangha

Although there is mention of three types of surrender, but they all merge into one, as each is dependent on the other.

The World
Though Buddhism reached Japan fairly late, it established very deep roots. Nara is the Holy City of Buddhism in Japan.

Thailand is known as the Land of the Buddhas, on account of the multiple Buddhist shrines and monasteries that are found there.

Religious Symbols
Early Buddhism abstained from pictorial representation of Buddha because he was adamant that there should be no veneration of the physical form, either in sculpture or in paintings. Therefore, symbols were used to express respect and veneration for the Buddha, such as his feet, a lotus, or the *Dharma Chakra* and the stupa. Later, the stupa became a basic model for all Buddhist architecture such as the Pagodas in the countries of the Far East. However, ultimately Buddhism did not hesitate in using the full figure of the Buddha and the *Bodhisattvas* for the purpose of religious homage.

The Wheel
In Buddhism, the Wheel is generally referred to as the 'Dharma Chakra', and is invariably shown with spokes. The Dharma Chakra represents the eternal law of karma, birth, and re-birth.

The Smiling Buddha

The most powerful symbol, however, is connected to the physical presence of the Buddha and that is the Smile of Nirvana. Nowhere in the Buddhist texts does the Buddha define the nature of Nirvana. The implication is that Nirvana cannot be described, it can only be experienced. When Nirvana is experienced, a human being blossoms with the smile of The Buddha, which is a smile of absolute tranquility, the smile of a person who is at peace with himself and the world.

The Lotus

The mystic mantra of Tibetan Buddhism is, *Om mane padme hum,* which means 'I revere the jewel in the Lotus.' The Ashoka Pillar depicts an inverted lotus. Buddha is often shown seated on a lotus. Buddhism took this common Indian flower, and added a new dimension to the Hindu religious symbolism that is associated with the lotus.

Throughout China and Japan, there is a tradition of respect amounting to worship which is shown to the spirits of one's ancestors. It is observed in Buddhist temples, where worshippers light lanterns, chant sacred texts, light candles, and offer fruits.

The monks play a very important part in Buddhism. The initiation of a young novice is an elaborate affair in the Eastern countries. A monk lives upon the generosity of the people who supply him with alms. The Buddhist Bhikku still goes around collecting food in his bowl. This asking for alms is not begging. This act of charity gives an opportunity to the giver to gain merit.

Now-a-days, we also find many Buddhist nuns. Probably in early times, women were not permitted to enter the Order.

It appears that Buddha had no patience with the abstract problems which so intrigued the Indian Brahmanical sages.

To Buddha, these frantic efforts to solve these riddles seemed pointless. His sole concern was with man and man's life here on earth and with 'misery and how to get rid of it.'

Activity Time
1) Why did Siddhartha give up a life of luxury to become a poor holy man? Do you normally prefer to take the easy way out and abandon your goal, or do you struggle and choose the difficult path, if required, to achieve your goal?
2) With reference to Siddhartha Gautam's life, do you think austerities alone can lead someone to Enlightenment?
3) Do the Four Noble Truths sound like sensible advice to you? Do you agree with them?
4) Do you think that the eight-fold path is realistic and can be followed in current times?
5) What do you find the most interesting in Buddhism?

JAINISM

ROOTS

Introduction

Trisala, the lovely princess was restless. She kept tossing and turning in her bed. In her troubled sleep, dreams chased one after another.

First, she saw a mighty white elephant. Then a white bull which was surrounded by a dazzling light. Next, she saw a magnificent white lion which leapt from the sky towards her face. She saw many wonderful things in her dreams, including Goddess Lakshmi, the white luminous moon, and the radiant sun. She woke up extremely perplexed. The king sought advice of the royal astrologers. They all foretold the birth of a wondrous son, who would become famous throughout the world.

Trisala was overjoyed. She prepared for the birth of her child, taking care of her health and mind. On the thirteenth day of the bright moon, in the month of April, Trisala gave birth to a lovely baby boy.

On the twelfth day after his birth, his parents named him Mahavira. He was also called Vaisaliya, the man from Vaisali.

To the world, he is best known as Mahavira, the great hero, or Jina the conqueror. Jainism derives its name from him. Many historians place Mahavira between 599 and 527 BCE. This was a period of great religious ferment throughout the East. It was a time when Confucius and Lao-tzu taught in China, when Zarathustra was preaching in Persia, when the great prophets of the Babylonian exile, Jeremiah, Ezekiel, and Isaiah were preaching to the Jews; at about this time, the early Greek philosophers were also searching for a new meaning of the universe and man's position in it.

Childhood

From his childhood, Mahavira longed to forsake the world and lead a wandering, ascetic's life. But he felt that he could not do this as it might cause pain to his parents. So, he lived the life of a normal happy child. He excelled in all things, in strength and physical endurance, as well as in intelligence. Legend tells us that one day, while he was playing with his friends, a mad elephant charged at the boys. Instead of running away like the rest of them, Mahavira caught the infuriated animal by its trunk, and tamed it.

Youth

According to the *Svetambara* tradition, Mahavira was married to a lovely girl called Yashoda. A daughter was born to them who was named Anuja or Priyadarshana. When Mahavira was thirty years old, his parents died. Now, he felt free to take up the life of an ascetic. He asked his brother's permission to renounce the world. His brother advised him to wait for another year, so that people would not think that the brothers had quarrelled. According to the Digambara sect, it was in his parent's lifetime that Mahavira became a *sanyasi* (monk).

Mahavira's Initiation

The *Naya* clan to which he belonged, followed the rules of Parsvanatha, an ascetic who had lived some two hundred and fifty years before Mahavira. In a park outside Vaisali, under the shade of the Ashoka tree, Mahavira made the great renunciation and entered the life of a monk. He fasted for two-and-a-half days, without taking a drop of water, and then gave away all his personal belongings and property. Legend tells us that he was carried to the park followed by a crowd of gods and men and took his place on a five-tiered throne facing the east. This kind of throne is called a *Pandusila* and in Jain temples, Mahavira's image is usually kept on one of these.

He then performed a most painful ritual. As proof of the power of endurance, Jains must tear out their hair by the roots. According to legend, as he tore out his hair in five handfuls, Indra, the king of gods, knelt before Mahavira and collected the hair in a priceless jewelled cup.

After this ritual, Mahavira took his vows of abstinence from sinful acts and adopted a holy life. It is said that Mahavira was born with three degrees of knowledge called *Mati Jñana, Srutha Jñana,* and *Avadhi Jñana.* Now, he gained the fourth degree of knowledge, *Manahparyaya Jñana* by which he knew the thoughts of all beings. After this, he only had to obtain the fifth degree of knowledge of Omniscience, which only the *Kevali* or a perfect person possesses.

The Digambaras believe that he obtained the Manahparyaya Jñana much later, after his initiation, but before that, he wandered about in the forest doing penance and intense meditation. At last, he visited Ujjain, and there he did penance in a cemetery. Rudra and his wife tried to interrupt his meditation and repeatedly tempted him. It was only after overcoming these temptations, and entering the forest as a recluse, that he obtained enlightenment.

Then Mahavira went about the country absorbed in meditation. He was untouched by sorrow or joy, pain or pleasure, and lived by begging for alms.

Mahavira Abandons Clothes

At first, it appears that Mahavira wore clothes or one piece of cloth for about thirteen months.

The question of wearing clothes was a very important one for Jains. Mahavira felt that to be a complete ascetic, one must conquer all emotions, shame amongst them.

He was indifferent to pain. One day, while he was meditating outside a village, some herdsmen in sport, lit a fire beneath his feet and drove nails into his ears. The saint was serene and not even aware that anything out of the ordinary had occurred.

Discipline

For twelve years, Mahavira wandered from place to place. He made it a rule not to stay longer than one night in a village and five nights in a town. The rule was relaxed during the rainy season, when he stayed for four months at the same place. It is still followed by his followers. 'He was pure like the leaf of a lotus and nothing could soil him. Like the Earth, he patiently bore everything and like a well-kindled fire, he shone in his splendour.'

Enlightenment and Death

Twelve years after his renunciation and years of wandering and penance, Mahavira stayed in a place called Trimbhakagrama, not very far from Parasnath Hills. One afternoon, the ascetic was sitting in deep meditation at a quiet spot under the shade of a Sal tree. As he had done previously, he fasted for two-and-a-half days without even touching water.

He was lost in contemplation and it was then that he attained supreme enlightenment and omniscience (*kevali*). His austerities and meditations had been so intense that all his past karmas were destroyed. Now he was free and became Jina (conqueror of the eight Karmas—the great enemies). He became an *Arhat* (worthy), *Arihanta* (destroyer of enemies), and *Aruhanta* (one who has killed even the roots of karma).

Mahavira's Message

Mahavira's first sermon was on the five great vows which are described later in this chapter. Mahavira's message to humanity was that birth and caste do not matter. Future happiness depends on the completion of karma.

After about a year of gaining Omniscience, Mahavira became a *Tirthankara* (a prophet or a person who guides mankind across the troubled ocean of life). The Jain leader had great capacity for organisation, and taught his religion to all. His chief message was universal brotherhood, and humanity, and he was against casteism. He was supported by the rich and the aristocracy.

For thirty years, he taught mostly in the Gangetic kingdoms, and was accepted with enthusiasm and honour by the ruling kings. He travelled with the monks and nuns who had entered the order. It is said that he converted many powerful states of northern India to Jainism which included Magadha, Bihar, Prayag, and Kausambi.

According to the Digambaras, the king of Magadha, Srenik, went with his whole army to receive Mahavira on his first entry into the country, to hear him teach. He was so impressed that he entered the order and became a staunch champion of Jainism. Wherever Mahavira went, he gathered people around him. He was much loved and admired. He even won over the members of the order of Parsvanath to which he had once belonged.

Death - 527 BCE

His end was now drawing near. He had travelled for thirty years, preaching and converting. He spent the last rainy season in Papa, a place in Patna district. Sitting in the *samparyanka* position, he delivered fifty-five lectures that explained the results of karma. Having finished his great discourse, he died and attained freedom from birth, old age, and death. Unaided, he had worked out his own salvation. The 'Two Terrible Ones' as the Jains called them, Birth and Death, had no power over Mahavira any longer. He had gained 'Nirvana.'

Shoots

According to the Jainas, the best way to begin the study of their history and how it spread is through the stories of the Tirthankaras. A Tirthankara is one who has attained 'a passionless and ineffable peace' and has made the passage across the ocean of worldly illusions. Tradition tells us about the first Tirthankara known as Risabhadeva or Adinath, who is also mentioned in the Vedas and the Puranas. He taught men about the Jaina faith. He had renounced his kingdom and had become an ascetic. After deep and prolonged meditation, he received the highest knowledge called *'kevala'*. 'Jainism is considered the oldest of non-Aryan groups and the religion goes back to the remote antiquity.'

Under Mahavira's influence, the religion spread and large numbers of men and women joined the order to escape from the trials and tribulations of this mortal life. Chief amongst his followers were fourteen thousand *munis* or monks. Renunciation of all things such as property, love, and emotions seemed a safe refuge.

The Jainas did not expand for about two centuries. A great schism arose in Jainism on the point of retention of nudity which Mahavira had established. Sthulabhadra, the leader in the North in the third century BC, allowed his followers to wear white garments to conform to the rules of the existing society. They were called *Svetambaras* (white-clad), and the other sect was called the *Digambaras* (sparse-clad or naked). There were never any fundamental differences in the doctrines, but the division is still present.

The rigorous austerities of Jainism found few adherents.

However, Jainism did not disappear entirely from the land of its origin. In fact, it was confined to India. This was partly because of the support given to it by the wealthy merchants and the middle classes. It is certainly a strange paradox!

Holy Books and Scriptures

The oldest scriptures of Jainism are the 'Agamas'. These are a collection of the sayings of the Tirthankaras.

According to tradition, an oral sacred literature was passed down from the days of Mahavira.

The Jaina monks were deeply interested in secular literature and other branches of learning and poetry. Owing to their love for literature, they laboriously and lovingly copied and illustrated not only religious manuscripts, but also secular ones. The Muslim invaders repeatedly destroyed many books by burning and looting temples, but later the Jaina monks started hiding them underground and thus saved many manuscripts, art, and rare articles.

Jainism like Buddhism is essentially atheist. It does not deny the existence of the gods, but it does not ascribe any important role to them in the universal scheme of things. According to the Jainas, the world is not the work of a personal deity, but functions on its own as per the laws of nature.

The Four Pillars of Faith

Mahavira said that there are four pillars of faith in the Jaina religion. These are:
Monk (*muni*)
Nun (*sadhavi*)
Layman (*shravak*)
Women (*shravika*)

Anekantavada

Jainism is not a fatalistic system. It has a remarkable theory known as 'the doctrine of manysidedness (*anekantavada*)'. This means to look at things from various points of view. In this way, it teaches us tolerance and understanding of other people's attitude. In the same way, a man has freedom to work out his own salvation.

Self-Purification

To be successful, control of speech, word, and act are called the 'three *danda*'. *Maunadharma* means speaking as little as possible, and keeping it to the point of avoiding telling falsehoods or hurting another person's feelings. Jainas are advised to remain in solitude and keep silence in the morning and evening, and if possible, the whole day. They believe that speech is silver, but silence is golden.

There are not more than two million Jainas in India. The great discipline of the lay community is one of the chief reasons for the survival of this faith.

The Jaina Creed

The Three Jewels of the Jainas are:
Right Knowledge *(Samyak Jñana)*
Right Faith *(Samyak Darshana)*
Right Conduct *(Samyak Charitrya)*

These three sum up the Jaina beliefs as expressed in their vows and rules of conduct.

Right Faith is necessary to gain insight into the Jaina scriptures, and to be able to believe, for without faith all conduct is worthless.

Jains believe in not harming or hurting anyone by speech, look, or deed. The heart and mind as well as actions should act in unison and do what should be done. This is a very important Jaina belief.

The Five Great Vows

Parasvanath had made four great vows that were binding on his followers:

(1) Not to take life (*ahimsa*)
(2) Not to lie
(3) Not to steal
(4) Not to own property, that means limiting your possessions to necessities, and curbing desires

Seeing the abuses in society, Mahavira added another vow:
(5) Vow of chastity: A monk should be celibate while a layman should be faithful to his spouse

Holy Men

There are twenty-four Tirthankaras (prophets), also called 'the great prophets'. They are credited with the formation of this faith and appear in every age (*kalpa*). These great teachers made individual contributions in the forming of the Jaina faith and philosophy. After attaining absolute knowledge, they were called *Kevalin* and this term is used specifically to describe a Jaina saint.

The favourite Tirthankaras are the first and the last three. The images of the others with their special symbols, are found in temples. The symbols are always found on the Jaina icons that represent them. For example, the hooded snake is the symbol for Parsva and that of Mahavira is a lion.

The names of four of the most popular Tirthankaras and their symbols are:
- The first Tirthankara is Rishabanatha or Rishabadeva—the bull
- The twenty-second Tirthankara is Neminatha—the conch shell

- The twenty-third Tirthankara is Parsvanatha—the snake
- The twenty-fourth Tirthankara is Mahavira—the lion

Holy Places
Worship
Jainism does not believe in a Supreme God who is the creator and preserver; therefore, there is no image to be worshipped. But as the common man wanted some object to fix his devotion on, the idols were introduced. It is presumed that worship of the images of the Tirthankaras was allowed in the belief that it was the 'Ideal Worship.'

Dilwada Temple

A Jaina temple is not built on any holy spot where some Tirthankara achieved enlightenment nor is it a memorial to some holy man. Instead, the Jainas selected picturesque spots for their temples which would help the worshipper to acquire tranquility and peace. All the Jaina sects do not have temples for worship.

Festivals, Rituals, Ceremonies, and Practices

The Jainas have their own festivals, rituals, and fasts which are distinctly Hindu in nature such as Diwali, Ganesh Chaturthi, and Rakshabandhana. The influence of Hinduism is felt more by the Jaina women than by the men.

The closing day of the Jaina year and of *Pajjusana*, called *Samvatsari* is the most solemn fast of all. At the close of a meeting, they all ask for forgiveness (*Kshama*) from each other and from friends, for any offence they might have committed knowingly or unknowingly. There is determination to start the New Year with love and charity; friends and relatives are also visited with the same request for forgiveness and understanding. This general act of penitence is followed by a day of rejoicing.

> **Practising Jainism**
> *Karma leads to great unhappiness for the person who obtains it. The karma resulting from good deeds is dissipated almost immediately; it does not help to wash out the bad karmas; it just does not add to the load of bad karmas. To escape birth and rebirth (transmigration), karmas must be exhausted by penance and fasting, and by observing certain strict rules and disciplines.*

Ahimsa or non-violence means purity of thought, word, and deed. It means universal love, compassion, and sympathy for all living beings, however, tiny or insignificant they might be. This doctrine was meant for the monks and the laymen. It expressed the sentiment that if you cannot give life, you have no right to take it. The Jainas must be complete vegetarians and should also avoid eating vegetables that grow underground as well as fruits and vegetables such as tomatoes, cauliflowers, and egg plants, which have seeds and are breeding grounds for microscopic insects.

The Jainas believe that human beings, animals, and insects all have souls.

For a Jaina, there are very limited avenues for livelihood. A Jaina should not be a farmer, as ploughing and tilling the earth involves harm to animal life, and disturbs the soil itself.

Even most crafts and industries are closed to the Jainas as they involve injury to living beings. The planks sawn by a carpenter suffer directly, a blacksmith gives pain to the metal on the anvil. Thus, for the Jaina, trade, money lending, and jewellery, as well as practising law and teaching are the safest professions.

The Jaina Monk

If the life of a Jaina layman is strictly organised, then that of a Jaina monk is even more rigidly disciplined. He has to renounce possessions and can only retain five garments, (three upper and two lower). The next step in the initiation is the removal of hair (locks) by tearing them out by the roots, at least once a year.

A Jaina monk is a homeless wanderer with no worldly possessions who depends solely on alms of the charitable for food. The rules and regulations for begging of alms are also

Jain ascetics keep their mouths covered to prevent injury even to the minutest insect in the air

very strict. They eat frugally, and live with great austerity and subject their bodies to severe penance, fasts, and prayers.

Nuns

The female ascetics (*sadhvi*s) are greatly revered by the Jainas and have an equal place along with men. Their lives are similar to the monks, with many limitations to their attire and food.

Ceremonies

The Jaina birth, marriage, and death ceremonies are similar to those of the Hindus. Socially, they are Hindus, but religiously, they are Jainas. Inter-marriage has always taken place in certain areas while customs and rituals are almost the same in both the faiths.

However, unlike the Hindus, the Jainas do not have *'shradha'* (remembrance) ceremonies for the departed souls.

Fasting with *tapa* or austerity, forms an important basis of the whole Jaina faith, and self-mortification is emphasised.

Activity Time

1) What was Mahavira like as a child? Why did he not become a monk in childhood? Do you always do and act as you want, or do you sometimes think of the other person's feelings before acting? Which is more gratifying?
2) Who or what is a Tirthankara? Have you ever met anyone like that (he or she may not necessarily be a Jaina)?
3) Do you think the Three Jewels of Jainism would be easy to follow in life?
4) How would you interpret Ahimsa?
5) What do you find the most interesting in Jainism?

SIKHISM

ROOTS

Introduction

Once, a young man was bathing in the River Bein, which flows through the districts of Hoshiarpur, Kapurthala, and Jalandhar now in the state of Punjab, when he inexplicably fell into a trance. According to tradition, he remained submerged in the water for three days, meditating, and had a mystical experience of being swept into the presence of the divine. His followers waited in suspense at the river bank, to hear what he would say. He came out, but was silent, and people wondered and waited with bated breath for him to speak. Then he declared: 'There is no Hindu nor Muslim, so whose path shall I follow? I shall follow God's path.'

The people were startled to hear this profound statement. Each man was certain of what he was, either a Hindu or a Muslim. What new theory was this man suggesting?

This man 'Nanak' started a new religion based on his vision of the human life and lived in constant awareness of God. He laid the foundation of the present Sikh Religion.

Guru Nanak

Nanak was born in 1469, in Talwandi in Punjab. He was a Kshatriya, and was brought up in a traditional orthodox family. His father was a tax collector for Rae Bular, the Muslim owner of their village.

Childhood

Nanak's childhood was spent in turbulent times. At that time, northern India was under Muslim domination where the Hindus and Muslims were engaged in acrimonious arguments about religion, rituals, and social behaviour.

Nanak learned both Sanskrit and Persian, and from an early age, God became his main pre-occupation. It is said in the *janam sakhis* (stories about Guru Nanak's life believed to have been written some fifty to eighty years after his death) that when questioned about his name, he always replied: 'My name is Nanak Nirankari (one who belongs to the One Absolute God).' His religious thoughts must have been influenced by the official monotheistic Islam of popular sufistic movements, brahmanic rituals, the bhakti followers (devotion to God), and the songs sung by such bards as saint (*Sant*) Kabir.

Social practices, especially rituals, which were not in harmony with religious ideology or thoughts were condemned by Nanak.

When he was sixteen, Nanak went to live with his sister at Sultanpur. She was married to Jai Ram, who was a steward to Daulat Khan Lodi. Nanak, who was very intelligent and honest, was employed as an accountant by the latter. He was married young, and had two sons, Sri Chand and Lakhmi Das.

Nanak, the Guru

Nanak was eager to find out more about God. At the age of twenty-seven, he set out preaching and visiting religious centres in India and travelled from Assam in the East, Sri Lanka in the South, to Tibet in the North. According to tradition, after a pilgrimage westward to Mecca and Medina and a visit to Baghdad, he settled down in Kartarpur with his family.

On his journeys, he took a Muslim musician called Mardana with him, who played his stringed instrument whilst Nanak sang the hymns that he had composed himself.

Nanak was very broad-minded, and disliked the narrow rituals that were practised in India at that time. Once, the Muslim Mardana accidentally went into a Hindu sacred place which was out of bounds for the lower castes and the Muslims. The Hindus were very offended, but Guru Nanak rebuked them by saying:

'Perversity of soul is like a drummer woman,
Lack of compassion like a butcher woman,
The desire to find faults with others
Is like a scavenger woman,
The sin of wrath is like an utter outcast;
What use is it to draw a line around your kitchen
If four such vices keep you company.'

His Preachings

Crowds flocked to hear him and learn from him. The members of the community observed certain daily routines of bathing and prayers. These prayers were composed by Guru Nanak himself and were called *Japji* in the morning, and *Sodar* and *Arti* in the evening. He started the ritual of community meals which is now known as *'guru ka langar'*.

The idea was that by eating together, the barriers of caste would be broken. He did not believe that birth and caste determined the status of man in society; instead, he advocated community service or *seva*.

In the *dharamsala* or hostel or resting places, Sikh men and women prepared food together and shared it with all who came there. Hymns were sung and it was also a place of worship. As practised by Guru Nanak and his followers, worship was simple and had few of the requirements of the Hindu rituals. However, worship was not to be practised alone, but in a congregation which was called *sadhsangat*. These places of worship were the forerunners of the 'gurudwaras' or doors that lead to the guru.

Sikh

The word 'Sikh' comes from the Sanskrit word *shishya*, and literally means to learn as is done by a 'disciple' or 'follower'. So, in this centre around Nanak grew a community of followers which was unique and which belonged neither to the Hindu nor Muslim faiths.

Guru is a well-known word in India and means a religious or spiritual teacher who is considered essential for a spiritual life. According to Nanak, a guru was described as 'the ferry across the ocean of existence.' A true guru reveals the divinity of man to the individual.

'To have access to God's *naam* (name), the guru is the ladder, the boat, the raft. The guru is my place of pilgrimage and sacred stream.' (*Adi Granth*)

'A guru is an ocean full of pearls. The saint swans pick up those ambrosial pearls.'

Sikhs believe that the guru is a central pivot of their faith. It applies to God, to human religious masters, the scriptures, and society. Many important names and key words begin with 'gur', such as:

'Gurmukhi', the script of the Guru Granth Sahib; 'Gurbani', the words of the Guru Granth Sahib; and, 'Gurudwara', the place of worship where the scriptures have been installed.

Nanak was given the title of 'Guru' by his successors. It means something special, not divine, but a messenger of God's words.

Guru Nanak chose one of his followers and not his son to take his place after his death. The title passed to nine successors, to the person who was spiritually most suited for the position. The nine gurus of the Sikhs were:

Guru Angad Dev
Guru Amar Das
Guru Ram Das
Guru Arjan Dev
Guru Hargobind
Guru Har Rai
Guru Har Krishna
Guru Teg Bahadur
Guru Gobind Singh

The last to be given the status of a living guru was the *Adi Granth or Guru Granth Sahib* (the holy scriptures of the Sikhs).

The Sikhs believe in the oneness of the Gurus:

'The same is the divine light, the same is the life form. The king has merely changed the body.' *(Adi Granth)*

Each guru was a physical extension of the last guru, and each contributed to the spread of Sikhism.

Guru Gobind Singh was the most important after Guru Nanak. He laid a detailed code of conduct to be followed by the Sikhs and founded the *'Khalsa'*. He also installed the holy scriptures, the Adi Granth or Guru Granth Sahib as the final guru to succeed him.

Guru Arjan Dev was instrumental in compiling the *Adi Granth* and the 2216 hymns attributed to him are the largest contribution to the *Guru Granth Sahib.* He consolidated the Sikh faith by building major shrines at Amritsar and Tarn Taran.

Death

Guru Nanak was greatly revered by all, Muslims and Hindus alike. When he died there was a quarrel between the two sects about his last rites, since the Hindus wanted to cremate him while the Muslims wanted to bury him. A *janam sakhi* says that eventually both Muslims and Hindus agreed that each party should place flowers on the body, so the next day the party whose flowers were freshest could claim the body. But to the surprise of all, the flowers of both parties were equally fresh, but there was no body. So, the Hindus cremated their flowers and the Muslims buried theirs.

Shoots
Sikhism in India

After the death of Guru Gobind Singh in 1708, the Sikhs suffered periods of persecution. It was under Maharaja Ranjit Singh that they prospered again and grew in strength, but they were mostly confined to Punjab and parts of North India.

For almost hundred years, Sikhs emigrated overseas from Punjab. Now, Sikhism is represented in all corners of the world by Punjabi migrants, and non-Punjabi converts.

Holy Books and Scriptures
Guru Granth Sahib
Maharaja Ranjit Singh did not attach much importance to the 'Guru Panth', and this weakened the power of the assemblies. The idea of the *Guru Granth* was strengthened, and this sacred book was personalised and given a place of honour at all important functions and religious occasions. It became the visible expression of Sikhism, and the spiritual authority of the community. Consequently, in a unique sense, Sikhism is a religion of the book.

The Holy Book is *'pragat guru ki deh'*, the manifested body of the Guru. The utterances of the Guru are known as *'gurubani'*. The book is full of exquisite poetry which is recited as a song in rhythm. It contains no history or mythology, but praises God which inspires the worshipper.

The *Mool Mantra* or the 'root verse' is the beginning of the book, and is a portion of the Japji or the morning prayer.

In the Gurudwara, the Holy Book is enthroned under a special canopy. When opened, it is placed on a special stand that is supported by cushions. A Khalsa member shows respect by waving a *chauri* (a fan made of yak tail hair). When not being used, the Holy Book is covered by a decorative cloth. No Sikh ceremony is performed unless the *Guru Granth Sahib* is present.

If the Holy Book is kept in the house, a room is set aside for the purpose, and the scripture is treated as the Guru himself. However, it is important to understand that the book is not worshipped although worshippers prostrate before it in reverence.

Mool Mantra

Guru Nanak's hymns, the *Japji Sahib*, is the keynote of the Sikh beliefs about God, and is recited by them in their morning prayers. It commences with the main prayer, which is a declaration of their faith:

God is one (*ik onkar*)
God's name is truth (*satnam*)
God is the imminent creator (*karta purakh*)
Without fear (*nirbhau*)
Without enmity (*nirvair*)
Immortal in form (*akal murat*)
Unborn and self-existent (*saibham*)
(Known by) The grace of the Guru (*gur prasad*)
(Adi Granth, first page)

Dasam Granth

The *Dasam Granth* written in Braj Bhasha, Persian, and Punjabi, was compiled by Bhai Mani Singh after the death of Guru Gobind Singh. The two main themes of Guru Gobind's works were aimed at filling people with patriotic enthusiasm, and martial fervour. His verses were meant to stir the people to fight against tyranny and fanaticism of Emperor Aurangzeb. He composed devotional songs, full of heroic grandeur and deep faith in God, which reflected his spiritual greatness.

The gurus wrote in a simple language which could be understood even by the illiterate people. They used popular sayings and current figures of speech to illustrate their ideas. To explain profound thoughts and philosophy, homely similes were used.

Characteristics of the Sikh Religion

Sikhism places its trust and faith in the absolute God, who is not bound by time and space. He is the Creator, Preserver, and Destroyer of the universe. Therefore, God is omnipresent and omnipotent. There are no other gods and goddesses to whom reference can be made, and God does not assume a human form to be subject to conditions of human life and time.

Sikhism attaches great importance to virtues like honesty, compassion, humility, loyalty, generosity, and patience, as embodiments of the divine qualities which identify human life as belonging to a higher order. Thus, spiritual development is emphasised as an integral part of human existence.

Therefore, in Sikhism, ethics and religion go hand in hand. It is only by living a life of purity with the name of God as a source of inspiration that man can ultimately hope to reach God.

The lives of the gurus are shining examples of how they lived their practical lives in the light of God. The Sikh religion emphasises that even a householder in the midst of cares and worries of life, can relate to God in a number of ways.

Therefore, renunciation and asceticism are not stressed in the Sikh religion.

Holy Men and Great Personalities

Guru Nanak established the Sikh religion, but after him, came nine gurus who contributed in their own way to the development of the new faith.

Guru Gobind Singh wanted to establish a martial group of Sikhs who would be able to defend their people from oppression. He proclaimed a code of conduct for all Sikhs, which made them proud of their faith.

A **Khalsa** takes five vows which have come to be known as the 'Five K's', because each begins with the letter 'K' in Punjabi.

The 'Five K's' are:

Kesh : Uncut hair and unshorn beard
Kangha : A wooden comb
Kirpan : A dagger
Kara : A steel bracelet
Kach : A stitched garment

The wearing of a turban is an important feature of the Sikh image which also distinguishes them from others.

The dress, the turban, and the five K's demonstrate the commitment of the Sikhs to their faith. The adoption of the title Singh for men, and Kaur for women, show that they belong to one large family, regardless of caste.

The Sikh identity is confirmed by four special rites and festivals in which the presence of the Guru Granth Sahib is necessary. Besides the naming, marriage, and funeral rites, the act of initiation is taken by many.

Non-Sikhs wishing to be converted to Sikhism and join the Khalsa, are admitted through the *Amrit* ceremony (*Khande di pahul*) and thereafter, receive Sikh names.

Some rituals are common and shared with the Hindus, but have no religious bias.

Like Hindus, Sikhs also cremate their dead.

Two other names for God as Guru or the true preceptor are used. *Satguru* means the true Guru and *Vahiguru* is the distinctive Sikh name for God, the wonderful teacher, the source of authority.

Ceremonies and Practices

The Sikh and the Hindus have several common festivals.

The Gurudwara, meaning the 'door leading to the Guru' is the Sikh place of worship or temple. What started as a place for religious congregation of Guru Nanak's followers, later took on other activities such as teaching Punjabi in the gurmukhi script. Then came the free kitchen (*langar*), and free accommodation for travellers. Soon the gurudwara became a community centre, where birth, marriage, and death ceremonies were performed.

Worship is informal in the Sikh religion. There are no set rituals. The Guru Granth Sahib is kept in a central place on a raised platform, under a canopy. After removing their shoes, the worshippers sit on the carpets with their heads covered, where men sit on the right and women on the left.

There is no professional priesthood among the Sikhs.

Sikhism is based on three pragmatic concepts—*Nam Japna, Kirt Karo,* and *Wand Chhakna.* These three concepts are significant as they centre around remembrance of God, earning one's living by honest labour, and sharing with the less fortunate.

Sikhs believe in monogamy and family life. For a Sikh, marriage is sacrament, not a civil contract. Divorce is a modern problem, and to face this, either party can apply for a divorce under the Hindu Code or the Civil or Special Marriage Act.

Activity Time

1) How can we serve others selflessly, following the example of Guru Nanak and other Sikh Gurus?
2) Like Guru Nanak, do you think it is important to treat everyone equally, regardless of their background or beliefs?
3) How can we ensure everyone feels respected and valued in their school or community?
4) How can we show courage in our daily lives, just as the Sikh Gurus did? Have you ever seen someone stand up for what is right, even when it was difficult?
5) Have you visited the Golden Temple? What do you find the most interesting in Sikhism?

☬ ☬ ☬

JUDAISM

A map showing places where biblical events have taken place, based on intensive research. However, the locations indicated can only be approximated.

ROOTS

Introduction

One day, Abraham was making a sacrificial offering when suddenly God appeared before him and said, 'Go from your country to the land that I will show you. I will make a great nation for you, and I will bless you.... And I will bless them that bless you, and curse them that curse you.... And by you shall all the families of the earth be blessed.'

Abraham dominates the Biblical account of the beginnings of the Israelite religion. Judaism is a religion that was willed by God for the foundation of the Divine Order, the fulfilment of the Divine purpose on Earth, and the establishment of the Kingdom of Heaven.

Abraham migrated from Ur of the Chaldees to Canaan, the Promised Land, around 2000 BCE. But he did not settle there because at that time, there was a famine in the land. The Jews were condemned to ten centuries of warfare, migration, and slavery. Finally, fleeing from Egypt under Moses, they began their forty years' trek back to the hills of Judea, before they could settle in the Promised Land.

Far into old age (according to the Bible, at the ripe old age of hundred) when Abraham had given up all hopes of having a child from Sarah, God suddenly blessed him with a son called Isaac.

Abraham, Isaac, and his son Jacob, are known as the 'fathers' of the Jewish people, just as their wives, Sarah, Rebecca, Leah, and Rachel are called the 'mothers' of Israel.

Jacob wronged his brother (Genesis 32) to gain favour of his old father Isaac, by pretending to be Esau the older brother. Being blind, Isaac blessed Jacob, thinking it was Esau. Jacob was found out, and had to run away in shame. He stayed at the house of Laban, his mother's brother, and fell in love with his cousin Rachel, who was very beautiful.

Laban made a pact with Jacob and forced him to tend his flock of sheep for seven years before he could marry Rachel. But at the end of the period, he tricked him into marrying the elder sister, Leah. Poor Jacob served again for another seven years, and after encountering great difficulties, finally married his beloved Rachel.

Years later, he thought of returning home. But a strange thing happened. God appeared before Jacob and said: (Genesis 32) 'Your name is Jacob, but you shall not be called Jacob anymore. 'Israel' shall be your name'. After that, Jacob took the name 'Israel' and the generations that followed were called 'Children of Israel', those who struggle for God.

Jews regarded God as being just and merciful, and they wanted to be like him—just and merciful. The point to remember is, till that time people worshipped many Gods. But now the Jews identified themselves with the One, unique God. They felt that there was an immediate and constant interaction between them and this Creator of heaven and earth.

Sojourn in Egypt

It was during Jacob's lifetime that the Children of Israel came to Egypt. The Jews lived there in peace for four hundred years.

But later, a Pharaoh came to power who was different. That is when the picture changed for the Jews. He enslaved the Jews and treated them inhumanly and cruelly and made them do heavy manual labour.

Moses was left by his mother in an ark of bulrushes and hidden near the river bank. The Pharaoh's daughter came down to bathe in the river, and seeing the ark with the child inside, took compassion on him. Strangely, the boy's own mother nursed him. When he grew up, the Pharaoh's daughter made him her son and gave him the name of Moses. But somehow, he retained his identity as a 'Child of Israel', and seeing the harsh behaviour of the Pharaoh towards the Jews, he opposed him. To escape the wrath of the Pharaoh, Moses had to flee from the land.

Moses felt that his people's need for freedom was not just a human emotion, but it was God's Will. He was commanded by God to return and take his people out of Egypt. He went to the Pharaoh and demanded that his people be released.

'Let my people go', he told the Pharaoh. But the Pharaoh refused and Egypt was visited by a series of plagues. Still the Pharaoh refused to give the Children of Israel their freedom. But when the first-born Egyptian children died, the Pharaoh begged Moses to take his people and go.

Inexplicably, the Pharaoh changed his mind and sent his war chariots after the fleeing Children of Israel. By divine intervention, the sea (the Sea of Reeds now called the Red Sea) parted to let them cross over to safety, while the pursuing

Egyptian forces were drowned. It is clear that the Jews were saved to fulfil the definite purpose of God (Exodus Ch. XIV).

God spoke to Moses at Mount Sinai and gave him the Ten Commandments. After that Moses had the task of moulding the ex-slaves into a united people.

The twelve tribes of Israel descended from the twelve sons of Jacob, who formed themselves into a loose kind of federation. Eventually, David bound the twelve tribes by a strong Central Government. David was regarded as an ideal king, the kind who could bring God's kingdom to Earth.

David's son, Solomon the Wise, was a distinguished king. He built the first temple in Jerusalem, and for several centuries, it was the most important place of worship. After Solomon's death, the Jews were split into two kingdoms, Israel in the North, and Judah in the South.

From the 8th to the 6th centuty BC. Israel had to bear onsloughts from Syria, Assyria, Egypt and Babylon. Their temple was burnt and the Jews were exiled.

Much later, the Jews returned to Jerusalem and rebuilt the Temple. It was at this time, that the life of the Jewish community revolved around the temple and was guided by priests.

The Jews in Modern Times

The Jews began a humanist movement to live in the modern world and be universally accepted.

Strangely, after facing so many trials and sorrows and humiliations, the Jews were subjected to anti-Semitic persecution in Germany and France in the late nineteenth century. A sick idea arose that the Aryans were a superior race, and the Semites, the Jews, were pseudo-biologically, the inferior race.

During World War II, between 1939 and 1940, six million Jews were eliminated by the Nazis in gas chambers or shot down mercilessly simply because they were Jews. One-third of the world's Jews population ceased to exist. The holocaust as it was called, tested the sanity, security, and faith of the whole Jewish community.

After the war, the Jews were granted their old homeland, the Promised Land of Israel. This was the Chosen Land, Palestine, which was promised to them by God, and now their aspirations and dreams of belonging to this land were fulfilled.

Through their suffering, God was indelibly burning a passion for freedom and justice in the hearts of the Jews, hoping that the rest of the world would learn a lesson from them.

In India, a big Jewish community was concentrated at Cochin. There have been Jews in India for over 2,000 years and they call themselves the Children of Israel.

Holy Books and Scriptures
The Torah
The Torah is the Divine instruction for the Jews and its chief purpose is to guide them in their everyday life. The Torah is a means of purifying men. The special message of Judaism is that God reveals himself to his people. God's revelation and the covenant at Mount Sinai together formed the Torah.

Through interpretations of the Torah, the priests and the first century Rabbis wielded very influential positions in Jewish life, especially in ceremonial life at home and in places of worship.

The study of the Torah is a commandment which is given several times in the Bible.

The Talmud is a vast collection of writings which contain the teachings of the Rabbis.

Bible

The Bible is the basis of the Jewish creed and life. It teaches the relation of God with man, and the laws that men should follow.

The Rabbis of the first century compiled the Jewish Bible known as the **Tanakh**. It comprises three parts:
Torah - Teachings
Neviim - Prophets
Ketuvim - Writings

The Hebrew Bible is a treasury of sublime thoughts. It gives moral and ethical laws, a scheme of life and points the way to goodness to establish fellowship with God. The central teaching is the supreme idea of faith in a just, merciful, and righteous God.

The Covenant

There was a Covenant between God and His people. It was not slavery or blind obedience; it was a way of a regular encounter with God. The Jews were chosen by God to be the 'Chosen People'. God had chosen Israel for special tasks to witness the truth or Revelation. He cares for His people, and He guides them. But He demands total allegiance, and He sets certain stipulations. If those rules are broken, then the Chosen People are punished. The Bible shows that Judaism is not only an intellectual or philosophical system, but is primarily a religious belief in the holiness, righteousness, and mercy of God.

Abraham

Abraham stands out in Jewish belief as one of the greatest of all the early patriarchs. He is known as the 'father of the faithful', and the 'friend of God.'

At the time of Abraham, in around 2000 BCE, his people believed in many gods. The forces of nature and the natural phenomena were all worshipped as gods. But when God called Abraham, and made Himself known to him as the one and only unique God, Yahweh, the latter believed him and followed His will unquestioningly.

Abraham and Yahweh made a pact wherein God agreed to accept the Hebrews as his chosen people and to take special interest in them. In return for His love and guidance, the Jews would follow a course of conduct in their daily lives which envisaged the happiness and well-being of their fellow men. An ethical pattern was woven into religion, along with rites and ceremonies.

Moses

After Abraham, the next great figure in Jewish history is that of **Moses**, who laid down the basic Biblical laws. But it was left to the Pharisees and the Talmudic scholars to interpret these laws. Hence, the term Rabbinic Judaism.

Moses is always associated with the Ten Commandments that were given to him by God on Mount Sinai, for the Jewish people to strictly obey and follow.

Jerusalem

Jerusalem is a sacred holy city to the Jews, and it personifies all their hopes and aspirations which made it bearable for their exile from their Chosen Land for almost twenty centuries.

After Christ, Jerusalem became a place of pilgrimage for the Christians. In 637 AD, it fell to the onslaught of the Muslims, and owing to its association with Mohammed, it was regarded as holy. Here, they built a mosque on the site of the temple.

After seeing many rulers, in 1948, the city was divided between the new State of Israel and the Kingdom of Jordan until its capture by Israel in 1967.

The sacred city of Jerusalem has seen bloodshed as no other city in the world. But surprisingly, this bloodshed has been in the name of religion—of Judaism, Christianity, and Islam—that Jerusalem has been ravaged and has seen crimes committed that are beyond comprehension.

The deep love and yearning for Jerusalem in Jewish hearts can be gauged by their greetings to each other, 'Next Year in Jerusalem'.

Rituals and Practices

The Temple was visited on important festivals, but eventually, the Synagogue became more popular. This is a unique institution. There is no altar, and no priesthood. It is just a place of popular education, a place of study, and worship.

Babies symbolise the survival and continuity of a family, thus a baby is brought to the synagogue and introduced to the people by its Hebrew name.

The Jews are very particular about the purity of the food that is eaten by them and that it is *kosher* (ritually fit according to Jewish dietary laws).

Every Jew is not particular about following their dietary laws. Some may not eat forbidden food but are not particular about keeping a kosher kitchen, either. Most of them reject pig meat, and all sea food that does not have fins and scales (such as shellfish, oysters etc.).

The *Sabbath* or the day of rest is a most important ritual in a Jew's life, and is very different from our Sunday. It lasts from sunset on Friday to sunset on Saturday. It has two basic 'events' which it commemorates. One is the creation of the universe by God with God's planned 'stopping'. The other is probably the release from slavery and exodus from Egypt. This was on the Sabbath.

One of the Ten Commandments reminds the Jews that it is very difficult to work without rest, so it is compulsory to give all servants and employees a day off. Thus, holiness, peace, and freedom are the basic ideas of Sabbath or *Shabbat*.

Day of Atonement: Yom Kippur

Ten days after the New Year comes this day of fasting and repentance. It is considered the holiest day in the Jewish Calendar.

Activity Time

1) 'The special message of Judaism is that God reveals himself to his people.' If you were lucky enough to meet God face-to-face, what would you say or do?
2) Why do you think that both the Jews and the Christians revere the Bible?
3) Jews are supposed to eat only Kosher food. Do other religions have similar restrictions? Research this.
4) Jews worship in a Synagogue. Do you know anything about it? Is there anything similar in any other religion?
5) The sacred city for the Jews is Jerusalem. Yet it has witnessed so much bloodshed. Why?
6) What is Sabbath? Does any other religion also prescribe a day or days of rest and prayer?
7) What do you find the most interesting in Judaism?

CHRISTIANITY

ROOTS

Introduction
A man was stretched between heaven and earth, his hands and feet were nailed to the cross. A crown of thorns pressed down upon his head. He looked terribly thin and worn, and his tongue was cleaved to his palate. The soldiers had ripped his garments and shared them as spoils, and they played a game of dice at his feet. Then a soldier hung a sign above the head of the Man. It read: 'Jesus of Nazareth, the King of the Jews.' Even in his agony, the Man whispered, 'Father, forgive them, for they know not what they do.'

The Birth of Jesus
Caesar Augustus, the Emperor of the Roman Empire, ordered a census of all the people in the cities of their ancestors. Joseph and Mary also travelled to the tiny town of Bethlehem for the counting. The town was overcrowded, and there was no place available for them to stay. Mary was approaching the time of delivery of her baby. With great difficulty, Joseph found shelter in a stable, and it was here that Jesus was born in a very ordinary way. Mary wrapped him in swaddling clothes and placed him in a manger.

But it was no ordinary event. The whole night lit up with a dazzling light, and Angels proclaimed His birth to the shepherds, 'A Saviour is born this day in the city of David, who is Christ the Lord.' The shepherds found the baby in the manger as foretold by the Angels, and told the amazed people what the Angel had said about the child. All glorified God.

The Three Wise Men

Around the time that Jesus was born (9 to 4 BCE), Judea was governed by an old and wicked king named Herod. When he heard that wise men had come from the East, following a star, and were asking for the one who was recently born as the King of the Jews, he was terrified. He consulted scholars and prophets of the day.

On learning that the Messiah had taken birth in Bethlehem, the cunning king sent for the wise men. While pretending to welcome them, he questioned them about the child, and made them promise to come back with word of the child's location, so that he too could worship the child. All this while, Herod was plotting evil against the child.

On the way to Bethlehem, a burning bright star appeared, and guided these three wise men to the abode of Jesus. They were overwhelmed with joy, and worshipped the baby, offering him gold, frankincense, and myrrh. After this, they were again warned by the same God who had blessed them with the star, not to return to Herod.

The Flight to Egypt

Joseph too was warned and fled with his family to Egypt. Herod was infuriated when the wise men did not return with news of the child. He commanded that every male child in Bethlehem who was two years old or younger, be put to death.

Thousands of innocent children were killed. However, Herod did not live much longer, and then Joseph was free to bring his family back to the land of Israel. The family came home to Nazareth in Galilee to raise the child.

Little is known about the life of Jesus from his infancy until about the age of thirty. The first that is heard about him is when he appears in a temple and confounds the priests with his knowledge. He was brought up as a carpenter, his father's profession, but he had a profound knowledge of the Old Testament scriptures.

The Jews, who were ruled by the Romans at that time, were unhappy, poor, and downtrodden. The Sadducees, a priestly class, co-operated with the Romans for their own benefit. However, the Pharisees were not interested in politics and were involved in the study and application of the Old Testament Law.

There were many Jews who resented the Roman rule. There were revolts and demonstrations from time to time against the foreign yokes, and the Jews hoped for the promised Saviour, whom God would send to save his people. At the time of Christ, hopes ran high and there were different versions of what the 'Messiah', the deliverer would be like. Some saw him as a spiritual figure while the majority expected a political liberator, a descendant of King David—'the King of the Jews'.

The Priestly Class
In those days, the priests were very rigid and superstitious in their outlook. They were more concerned with external rules

than in observing purity of heart, and morality. They were materialistic rather than spiritual or ethical, and despised the minority groups or non-Jews who were called Gentiles. They were afraid of new ideas which could threaten their Jewish religious establishment. Their rituals and heartless legalism and monopoly of interpreting the Old Testament Law gave them unquestioning power over the ordinary Jews.

The Sadducees had even turned the temple, on which their national religion was centred into a marketplace for buying and selling and profit making. In other words, the worship of God had become secondary, wherein 'The House of Prayer' had become a 'den of thieves.'

Jesus and His Public Ministry

It was in this climate of unrest, that Jesus took birth and grew up. But it was John the Baptist, who launched him on his public ministry. It was John, whose voice went up in the wilderness, crying 'Repent' for the kingdom of heaven is not far away. 'The kingdom of God is at hand.' This is the central theme of the Christian religion, that man must atone for his sins, and seek the Love of God to help him out of his misery. In the Jordan River, John baptised a grateful and eager crowd, and prepared them for the coming of the Messiah.

In the words of Prophet Isaiah, John declared, 'Make straight the way of the Lord'. Then a strange thing happened. Jesus went up to John to be baptised, and when he came out of the water, the spirit of God descended upon him in the form of a dove. A voice from heaven declared, 'You are my beloved son. In you am I well pleased.'

The Temptation of Jesus

For forty days and nights, Jesus wandered alone in the wilderness, never eating. He grew hungry. And then, at the end of that time, the devil came to him and tempted him with food.

But Jesus said, 'It is written Man shall not live by bread alone, but by every word that proceeds from the mouth of God.'

Again, Satan tempted him, and Jesus replied, 'You shall not tempt the Lord your God.' Once again, Satan tried and offered him the kingdoms of the world, but Jesus said: 'Satan, get out of my sight. You shall worship the Lord your God, and Him alone shall you serve.'

Defeated, the devil departed, leaving Jesus alone. The Angels came and comforted him for he was hungry and very tired after this ordeal.

Jesus travelled to Galilee with a handful of followers, to begin his ministry.

Jesus with his 12 apostles. (A painting by Masaccio around 1427)

Healing and Preaching

Jesus went into the towns and villages of Galilee and with astonishing authority, began to preach: 'The kingdom of God is at hand. Repent and believe in the good news.'

He was a good and magnetic speaker, and knew how to use words that appealed to the crowd. His preaching was a bright glorious experience, and seemed to the Jews like a light illuminating the black night of their lives. He spoke with power and sincerity and had charisma. He stunned his audience by saying in the synagogue:

'The spirit of God is upon me. The Lord has appointed me to preach the good news. I have come to heal the broken-hearted and the ill.'

Some of the audience was offended and shouted at him. But he said that 'A prophet is not without honour except in his own country and in his own house.'

He and his disciples deliberately chose to wander about the country, accepting hospitality when offered. He frequently spoke of the danger of becoming attached to worldly possessions.

Everywhere he went, he drew huge crowds. People were eager and came to listen to his words, and to receive the blessings of his hands. From the beginning of his ministry, Jesus was well-known as a healer. He touched the people and by a simple word, healed their diseases. He relaxed the limbs of the paralysed, straightened the legs of the lame, and cast out demons. There was no elaborate ritual, just a loving look or touch.

Everyone wondered at the miracles performed by Jesus. But many denounced him as a dangerous man.

Most of the recorded miracles are about healing, but he also displayed supernatural powers over nature. Now, Jesus began to choose men who would follow him more closely, learn from him, and would believe in him. He chose twelve out of his followers, and these were called his Apostles.

The growing popularity of Jesus, his radical views, and his sympathy for the poor and needy, aroused opposition from the leaders. His unconventional approach to the rules laid down by the priestly class was a threat to their authority. Therefore, the leaders vowed to silence him. His popularity with the masses dwindled because he declared he was not a political Messiah and would not be their king in their rebellion against Rome.

Death
At the Passover festival, Jesus rode into Jerusalem on a donkey. An enthusiastic crowd greeted him and hoped that he would announce himself the 'King of Jews', their earthly deliverer. But Jesus showed no interest in acting against Rome. He upbraided the religious authorities for their unscrupulous behaviour, and spoke against the temple regime.

Judas' (Judas Iscariot, one of the disciples of Jesus) greed for money caused him to betray his Master Jesus. This treacherous act earned him thirty pieces of silver.

Jesus was tried according to the Jewish Law for Blasphemy, as he claimed to be the Son of God, the Messiah. He was sentenced to death, but to make this effective, the permission of the Roman authority was necessary. The Roman Governor Pontius Pilate, wanted to have nothing to do with this, and so he publicly declared, 'I wash my hands off him'. Still the religious leaders caused him to be sentenced on charges of sedition.

Jesus carried his cross, and was crucified in the company of a robber and a murderer. On the cross, he signalled to John the Apostle to take care of his Mother Mary, and said: 'Woman, behold thy son'. Then in great agony he said, 'My God, my God why hast thou forsaken me'. And then in a note of triumph, he cried out, 'It is accomplished'.

His followers obtained his body, and buried it in a nearby tomb. To their utter astonishment, two days later, they found that the tomb was empty.

Resurrection

We read in the Gospels that Jesus repeatedly appeared to his disciples after his Resurrection. He was real, he ate and drank with them, and was no ghost. He explained to them the meaning of his life and death, and the mission they had to carry out. Then blessing them, he ascended to heaven.

Now, they began to understand his teachings and his mission and preached to the world that Jesus triumphed even over death, and was the Lord and Saviour. It is the Resurrection of Jesus which formed the focus of the earliest Christian

(The Resurrection, (Pinturicchio, 1492-94 at the Vatican Museum)

preaching and it was the risen Lord that they worshipped. This statement is the core of Christianity.

Fifty days after the death and Resurrection of Christ, the disciples were filled with the Holy Spirit and wisdom; they understood their mission. From that day onwards, the disciples started preaching about Jesus and the Kingdom of God. In the words of Peter, 'For the Lord God said, I will in the last days pour out my spirit upon all flesh. And it shall be that whoever calls upon the name of the Lord shall be saved.'

Spreading the Faith

In the beginning, the early Christians or followers of Christ, as they came to be called, preached only to the Jews. But soon the Apostles, and the messengers of faith spread the gospel of the good news of Jesus to the ends of the world, and 'to make disciples of all nations'.

The political and intellectual leaders looked at this new religion with disdain and distrust and as a challenge to their authority. The Christians were persecuted, and they became scapegoats when calamities occurred. But the more they were persecuted, the stronger grew their faith in Jesus Christ. They believed that they were sharing the sufferings of Jesus, and their faith would be rewarded.

By 60 AD, about thirty years after the crucifixion of Jesus, the new followers were living in Rome, perhaps also in Spain, France, and India.

The Roman Catholic Church

It is said that the Roman Catholic Church was founded by Peter, one of the disciples of Jesus. He was the first Bishop of Rome, the official title of the Pope. Today in the Vatican City, an independent state within the city of Rome, the Roman Catholic Church functions as the authoritative voice of the Roman Catholics all over the world.

The Protestant Church

By the beginning of the sixteenth century, Christianity was firmly entrenched as a major religion in all parts of Europe. But it was not all smooth sailing for the organisations of the Church. The authority of the Pope was frequently challenged because the Pope was also exercising political and economic control. Many people thought that the Pope should restrict himself only to spiritual matters. This led to large-scale protests and a demand for the Reformation of the Church. In course of time, there came about an organisation known as the Protestant Church.

Christian Church organisations grew in large numbers in many parts of the world, but they differed from the early churches in their practices and forms of worship. These included the Orthodox, Pentecostal, Methodist, Anglican, Baptist, and United Reformed Churches.

The Philosophy and Teachings of Jesus

Jesus spoke convincingly with bold authority, and his teachings which are recorded in the Bible, were principally oral.

Love for Humanity

Jesus stressed the dignity of man, spoke of forgiveness and did not believe in class barriers.

He was unique as a preceptor and teacher because he was full of love for humanity, and had a special quality of joyous affection for all, even for the sinners. He believed that the sin should be despised, not the sinner. His openness and acceptance of every kind of person, rich or poor, caused him to be criticised by the priests. His parables reflect the goodness that can be found in the lowest and the humblest.

Brotherhood of Man

The concept of 'Brotherhood of Man' arose from Jesus' conviction that all human beings are the children of God. He is the 'all loving' Father of mankind, and all are equal in His eyes. By example, Jesus also showed that men should care and help each other in sorrow and in distress, and should have sympathy for the less fortunate.

Jesus stressed again and again that the Kingdom of God is not found anywhere except within man. But to be worthy of this place in the Kingdom of God, the man has to first strive hard.

Jesus sought to explain that 'It is only by love and faith will man become truly whole and conquer his baser instincts.'

Holy Books and Scriptures
The Old Testament
The first part of the Bible are the Jewish scriptures, and they deal with the relationship of God with the people of Israel upto the time when Jesus came as the 'Messiah.' They are the Hebrew and Aramaic scriptures of Judaism, and are known as the 'Old Testament.' They contain a detailed history of the Jewish people.

The New Testament
This consists of twenty-seven books. They provide the only available record of the life and teachings of Jesus.

The Bible
The Bible is a collection of books written over a long period of time, about a thousand years. The word 'Bible' comes from the Greek word *Biblia*, which simply means 'The Books.' These books were written in different languages, and in different cultural and historic situations.

The Bible inspires us and is often called the 'Word of God.' It is not only a great spiritual work, but is also a source of enlightenment from God.

All Christians accept the authority of the Bible in forming their beliefs. The Christian faith is based on the Bible.

Festivals

Christmas is a very joyous festival as it celebrates the birth of Jesus on 25 December. Interestingly, this date was chosen by Emperor Constantine to coincide with the Roman Sun Festival, as the exact day when Jesus was born is unknown.

Easter is another important festival for the Christians, as it celebrates their central belief, the trial, death, and resurrection of Jesus.

Good Friday is the day Jesus died on the cross. It is called 'good' because it shows the 'goodness' of Jesus who undertook suffering on behalf of humanity.

Baptism is regarded as an outward, physical sign of rebirth, and the water symbolises the washing away of sin from human life. The verse used for Baptism by all Christian Churches is, *'I baptise you in the name of the Father, and of the Son, and of the Holy Ghost, Amen.'*

Protestants, however, hold a service, in which the young declare their belief in their faith. After this, they are blessed by the Bishop (the highest official under a senior member of the clergy), and are received into full membership of their Church.

Death

Christians are mostly buried, and mourners gather to pay their respects to the departed. The priest says prayers for the comfort of the dead and the living. An important belief is that the faithful will live with Christ after death.

Confession
In the Roman Catholic Church, a confession is heard in strict anonymity of the two parties, and it is confidential. The priest advises the confessor to repent and reform.

Trinity
Christians believe that not only was Christ God, but that God is a Trinity, consisting of the Father, the Son, and the Holy Spirit.
None of the Trinity is greater or lesser than the other, as there is one God in the Trinity, and the Trinity is in Unity.

Symbols
The Crucifix or **the Cross** is the most important symbol of Christianity. It can either be a plain cross, or can have the image of Christ as he was crucified. Priests and nuns, or for that matter, anyone can wear the crucifix around their neck, or carry it in their hands. In the earlier ages, the Cross also symbolised Holiness, and was supposed to ward off evil (Satan).
Sign of the Cross. This sign is the acknowledgement of God. It is made in the name of the Father, and of the Son, and the Holy Ghost. The priests make it to bless a person or a house. At the end of prayers, the priest dismisses a congregation by making this sign of the cross as a form of blessing.
Mary or Virgin Mary, or the Mother of Jesus, is a beloved

figure especially for Roman Catholics. She has a unique place as she is regarded as the link between earth and heaven. Being the Mother of Jesus, she can intercede on behalf of the devotees.

The Meaning of Christianity

What does Christianity mean to Christians? The followers of Jesus were called Christians because they were those 'who followed the way.' Christ's followers believed in Jesus as the Saviour and Messiah because then all sins would be forgiven and one could enter into a close relationship with God.

The Christians believe that with the banishment of Adam and Eve from Paradise, everyone is born in sin and will ultimately be saved from sin by Jesus, the son of God. Sin occurs when man transgresses the laws and commands of God.

Thus, the core of the religion lies in the fact that life, death, and resurrection of Jesus redeems people, gives them a new life, and reconciles them with God in a close and special relationship.

Thus, Jesus was both God and man. He is unique as he is the Son of God. Jesus always referred to Him as his Father. He and the Father existed together. Jesus came down to earth to save human beings, and was incarnate, that is, he became flesh and blood by being born like everyone else. He lived by what he taught. He lived a life of truth and was perfection itself.

Above all, Christianity emphasises a personal devotion to Christ who suffered for the sake of humanity. Thus, salvation for mankind is expressed in the person of Jesus Christ. All Christians find hope, love, and faith in Jesus, and they live their religion by experiencing these eternal values.

Activity Time

1) Why were the leaders and the Jewish priests hostile to Jesus? This is a common theme in the history of mankind—hostility against a new idea, faith, belief, or religion. Why do you think this occurs?
2) On the cross Jesus says, 'Father, forgive them; for they know not what they do.' Is forgiveness an important or an irrelevant virtue? Why do you think so? Are you able to forgive people who have wronged you?
3) Jesus performed miracles as did many other founders of religions and holy men. Why do you think they do this?
4) Is the Christian Trinity the same as the Hindu Trinity? Explain. What is the connection with the Cross?
5) Where is the Vatican? Is it important for all Christians?
6) Name three virtues taught by Christ.
7) What do you find the most interesting in Christianity?

ISLAM

ROOTS

Introduction

A man was spending a night alone on the Hira Mountain. He was asleep when suddenly, an Angel came to him with a piece of material and said, 'read it'. The man replied that he could not read. The Angel pressed the material so hard against the man, that he thought he would die. Then the Angel released him and said again: 'Read'. The command was repeated once more. Nervously, the man asked what he was supposed to read. The Angel said, 'Read in the name of your Lord, He who created, and made man from an embryo. Read, for your Lord is merciful like no one on Earth. He who instructed man by the pen, He taught him what he did not know.'

The man awoke from his sleep and stood as if in a trance. Then he heard a voice calling to him from heaven, saying, 'Mohammed, you are God's messenger, and I am Gabriel.'

The man looked up and saw the Angel on the horizon. Even when he looked away, he could still see the Angel. This was how Mohammed Ibn Ishaq recorded the event that occurred in the Prophet's life, and which was to so significantly affect the history of the world.

Islam is the name of the religion (surrender to God) that is practised by Muslims. The Muslims believe that Islam as a religion was brought to the world by Adam, and God sent his messengers to different regions at different times, to purify this religion and preach it. Mohammed came last and gave the final shape to the religion which already existed.

Mohammed: His Childhood
Mohammed was born around 570 AD in Makkah (Mecca) in a country which is now known as Saudi Arabia. His father's name was Abdullah (servant of God) and his mother was Aminah (serene/peaceful). They belonged to the Quraish tribe.

At that time, Mecca was a prosperous centre of the caravan trade between the countries bordering the Indian Ocean and the Mediterranean. Ka'ba was a sacred sanctuary, an ancient pilgrimage centre, which made Mecca prosperous, and encouraged trade. But prosperity led to social tensions, especially among the younger men.

Mohammed's childhood was one of sorrow and loss. He was a posthumous child, born after his father had passed away. When he was tiny, his mother asked a woman called Halima, who lived in the desert to care for the frail child, hoping that the fresh air would make him stronger. Aminah died when Mohammed was six years old.

His Early Life
A very interesting tradition tells us how Mohammed was prepared for his future work. Two angels are believed to have taken out his heart, cleaned it, and put it back. They weighed him on the scales but finally declared that 'were the whole

community to be weighed on one side and Mohammed on the other, he would still outweigh.' At first, he was looked after by his grandfather, and later at the age of eight, he went to live with his uncle, with whom he apprenticed as his camel driver. From the age of twelve, he travelled far and wide and saw and learned much of the world.

Subsequently, he was employed by a wealthy widow called Khadijah to look after her business and trade. Impressed by his integrity and success, she married him. At that time, she was forty while he was only twenty-five. Three daughters survived from this marriage and they were with him in his later years. In all, Mohammad had eleven wives and seven children. Unfortunately, all his children except Fatima died during his lifetime.

Messenger of Allah

Being secure in business and free from worldly cares, Mohammed developed contemplative habits.

In the revelations, Mohammed is sometimes spoken of as a messenger of God, and sometimes as a forecaster, warning sinners of retribution from God if they did not amend their sinful ways. He sincerely believed that these revelations were the words of God, which were revealed to him by an Angel, and they were not his compositions. Till today, Muslims believe this to be true.

The State of the Society

The Arab world comprised of many nomadic tribes who worshipped many gods and goddesses. Undoubtedly, many of them were familiar with the Bible and even read the Testament in Hebrew. But there seems to have been some unconscious acceptance of a Supreme Deity called 'Allah.'

In his fortieth year, something happened which changed the course of not only his life, but of millions of people. He received the call to proclaim the worship of One God (Allah). He received a messages frequently for some time, and was finally told to convey to his fellow Meccans, the Will of Allah and how they should live.

Mohammed and His Mission
At first, very few people believed that Mohammed was a prophet. His followers were known as Muslims which means they 'gave' themselves to Allah in peace.

Mohammed also spoke of the resurrection of the dead and of God's judgement. 'God will judge you according to your works', he told the town's traders.

The Meccan merchants violently opposed this religion which spoke of only One God and denounced the pagan gods. Soon, Mohammed and his followers were forced to live in a ghetto.

The persecution and hostility of the traders made it impossible for Mohammed to preach in Mecca. Therefore, he emigrated with his friends to Medina, a fertile oasis. This migration, the *Hijrah* became the event which is the beginning of the Islamic era or calendar (1 AH - After Hijrah).

At the invitation of some inhabitants who had become Muslims the previous year, Mohammed settled in Medina as the governor of the city. The people there accepted Mohammed as the Prophet.

After a year or two, the pagan Meccans started raiding Medina to attack the Muslims residing there. The Meccans outnumbered the Muslims in Medina both in terms of number of soldiers and equipment. But after prolonged battles spread over seven years, Mohammed's men, called *Zakhat*, were finally victorious and they took Mecca in 630 AD. His success and power were now established, and Mohammed became the unquestioned head of the state.

Entering the Ka'ba in Mecca, he smashed the idols. From then on, Islam was no longer just a religion but began to develop into a distinct political power. Mohammed was the head of the community of believers, who developed the Islamic social and religious practices.

Two years later, in 632 AD, Mohammed died.

His first successor was Abu Bakr who had been the first to accept Islam; he was also Mohammed's father-in-law and best friend and had often guided the community when Mohammed had been unwell. The loose federation of tribes or clans, now became more organised and Mohammed's 'successor' or deputy became the head of the State, and came to be known as the 'Caliph.'

After two more Caliphs, came Ali (the gate of learning). He was married to Fatima, the Prophet's daughter and was now appointed the Caliph. Hasan and Hussein were his two sons. He did not achieve much, and could not hold the Muslim community together. He was assassinated in the holy month of Ramadan and with him the line of 'rightly guided caliphs' ended in 660 AD.

Most religions usually grow slowly, but Islam spread with the speed of a hurricane. Muslims, all over the world, profess the same beliefs, utter the same prayers, turn their faces towards the same Holy city of Mecca. For these believers, it were these things that made Islam the Kingdom of God on Earth. Moreover, all are equal in Islam.

Most people of these countries did not convert to Islam at once. There were military expeditions (Holy wars) and the protected minorities were treated well. However, the minorities felt that they were second-class citizens, and over the centuries, there was a steady trickle of converts to Islam.

As European industrial technology developed in the nineteenth century, the Muslim rulers also wanted their countries to have railways, electricity, plumbing, telephones, and other modern comforts and conveniences.

However, it is interesting to note, that although the Muslims have adopted the western style of living and education, they are still very strict in observing their religion and Islamic laws.

Holy Books and Scriptures

Qu'ran, the sacred book of the Muslims, is derived from the Arabic word, Qu'ran which means 'to recite.' It is a revelation from Allah, and is not a collection of ideas from Mohammed the Prophet. Muslims believe that the Qu'ran always existed from the beginning of time and it was originally engraved on a tablet but was deposited by Allah in heaven. It was the Angel Jibreel (Gabriel) who revealed it to Mohammed and commanded him to recite it again and again.

Muslims try to memorise the whole book in Arabic, and those who do so are honoured by the title of *Hafiz*. During the five daily prayers, the Muslims repeat, in short, the first chapter of the Qu'ran in Arabic.

It was the first Caliph, Abu Bakr, who put together the various verses of the Qu'ran. Great care was taken to prevent mistakes or changes in the Qu'ran. Most of the book is in the form of the words of Allah which Mohammed was commanded by the Angel to repeat, until he knew them perfectly. Not only were the contents of the Qu'ran revealed, but also its order. They are not organised subject-wise or chronologically, but are a collection of verses that have been gathered over a period of twenty-three years in Mohammed's life.

The Qu'ran is divided into 114 *surahs*, or chapters. Most of the surahs start with the words, 'In the name of God, the Merciful, the Compassionate.'

The word 'Islam' means 'submission to God,' and a Muslim lives his life according to God's Will. Down the centuries, a Muslim has been taught what he should believe, and the sacred law directs him to behave according to the Islamic way of life, which is the core and kernel of Islam.

Hadith refers to the traditions which have been passed down by word of mouth about the sayings and doings of the Prophet. The Law of Islam, called the ***Shariat***, is based on divine revelations of which the main sources are:

The Qu'ran, which is believed to have always existed in Heaven, but was gradually revealed to Mohammed by the Angel Gabriel.

The Sunnah or practice or habit or custom refers to the Prophet's way of life, especially in countless traditions of what he said or did as a Prophet. Things like the way in which he prayed or fasted or washed before prayers was a guide to the Muslims, and is the basis for Shari'ah Islamic Law.

The importance of the Shariat lies in the fact that it is a divine commandment which governs everyone—from the highest to the lowest. Thus, God's commandment is strictly followed in the interpretation and application of these laws.

Mohammed's Concept of Allah
Mohammed regards God as the Creator and Restorer of all things. He is a mighty force who directs His sincere servants along the right path.

God is all powerful, omnipotent, omnipresent, and omniscient. All men and all creatures are subject to His all-pervading Will. Man's actions are determined by the Will of God, and transgressors are punished. God is compassionate, merciful, and loving. By living in the shade of these attributes, Man should extend these qualities to his fellow human beings.

Holy Places and Festivals
Jerusalem
Jerusalem is ranked behind Mecca and Medina in sacredness. Muslims believe that the great limestone outcropping within the mosque is sacred. From this rock, Prophet Mohammed ascended to heaven on his famous night journey.

Ramadan: To appreciate the hardships of the poor who go hungry, Muslims do not eat or drink during the day for one month. This teaches them self-control. It was on the twenty-seventh night of this month that Mohammed received revelations, and it is called 'The Night of Power.'

Id-Ul-Fitr: This is a festival of joy, which marks the end of the one month of fasting.

Haj: This is an Arabic word which means to 'set out with a definite purpose.' It takes place in the twelfth month of the Islamic calendar, and it is the ambition of each devout Muslim to go to Mecca at least once in their lifetime, if not more often. Only Muslims can enter Mecca and they all approach the sacred city as members of the same family. They all wear the same seamless white garments, through which all barriers of class and race are forgotten. They also converge to the Holy Black Stone or *Ka'ba* to say their prayers.

Muharram: This is observed around the month of August by Sh'ite Muslims. It commemorates the murder of Hussein, the son of Ali, and the grandson of the Prophet.

Rituals

Worship: 'I created humankind only so that they might worship me.' Every Muslim is taught this from childhood as a saying of Allah in the Qu'ran.

Shahada: The first pillar of Islam is *'shahada,'* the testimony of faith. It is a commitment to obey God, and follow the Prophet. 'I bear witness that there is no God but Allah. I bear witness that Mohammed is the Apostle of Allah.'

These words are breathed into a child's ear at birth and these are the last words which a Muslim whispers at his end. The words confirm his faith in Allah.

The Shari'a

The Shari'a further codifies and explains the practice of worship.

A Muslim has to pray five times during a day, and he prepares himself for it by the ritual of washing. These prayers are done at dawn, mid-day, mid-afternoon, sunset, and at night. Around the world, the worshippers unite in prayer and face towards Ka'ba in Mecca, taking care that each person is close to the next.

The Muslims follow the lead of the *Imam*, the prayer leader, and pray as a single body, reciting the prayer from the Qu'ran.

The third pillar of Islam is almsgiving called *'Zakat'*, which is the duty of sharing one's wealth with the poor.

Mosque (Masjid)

The prayer hall in a mosque (masjid), has no fixed pews or chairs but there are a number of prayer mats. The direction of Mecca is pointed out by the decorations or a plaque on the wall to make it different from the other walls. Usually, there is a table near the *mihrab*, or a platform which can be reached by a short flight of stairs. It is from here that the Imam (prayer leader) preaches. The men sit in the front while the women either sit at the back, or are segregated.

Outside the mosque is a minaret, from which the *muezzin* (who is chosen for his clear and loud voice) calls the Muslims for prayers five times a day.

There are no statues, images, or pictures of Allah or Mohammed inside the masjid as it would then be considered idolatry. However, masjids are sometimes elaborately decorated with abstract patterns or beautiful inscriptions.

Ceremonies and Practices

Marriage: No marriage is complete without the giving of dowry (*mehr*) to the bride which consists of money or property. Only a portion is paid to her on marriage, while the balance can be paid later when the husband dies or divorces her.

A Muslim man can marry a Christian or Jewish woman but the children have to be raised as Muslims. On the other hand, a

Muslim woman is not supposed to marry outside her religion.

According to the Qu'ran, a man can marry more than one woman at a time, the limit being four at any given time. The only condition placed is that the husband should treat all his wives alike, strictly on an equal footing.

Divorce: In several passages in the Qu'ran, the right of a husband to repudiate his wife by merely declaring his

Muslims praying at an Id gathering at Jama Masjid, Delhi, India.

intention of *talaq* (divorce) without intervention of the court has been affirmed. A triple repudiation made at one and the same time also constitutes a divorce, and is acceptable by all legal schools. Though, a wife has restricted rights and cannot divorce her husband by declaration, but by agreement she can have the marriage rescinded, by paying him compensation or by returning her dowry.

Food: Muslims are not allowed to eat pork or carnivorous animals. *Halal* is the special method of slaughtering the animal which has to be eaten. Drinking alcohol is prohibited.

There are two basic groups in Islam, the Sunnis and the Shi'as.

Sunnis: About 90 per cent of the Muslim community comprises of Sunnis.

Shi'as: The Shi'a Muslims believe that the Imam is the main figure of religious authority. Mohammed instited the cycle of initation, for guiding the community by appointing an imam as his successor. The first imam was Ali. It was after the martyrdom of Ali, who was not only Mohammad's adopted son, but also his son-in-law (by marriage to Fatima) that Shi'a Islam began.

Sufis: The Sufis are a special class of simple people who lead isolated lives and concentrate on meditation and prayers.

Activity Time
1) Who is the last Prophet of Islam?
2) What is the meaning of the words, Muslim and Islam?
3) Why did Mohammed have to flee to Medina? Why is it considered an important event?

4) Is Mohammed equal to God? According to Islam why did God create humans?
5) Zakat is necessary for all Muslims. Do you think it is necessary? Relate it to Corporate Social Responsibility.
6) What are the two basic groups in Islam. Find out which of these two is more popular in India.
7) Can you name some countries where most people are Muslims?
8) What do you find the most interesting in Islam?

CONFUCIANISM

ROOTS

Introduction

A venerable man was passing through the lonely countryside of Mount Li in China. He was accompanied by his disciples. Suddenly, he heard a woman crying. He stopped to ask the woman why she was crying. She said, 'My husband's father was killed here by a tiger, my husband too, and now my son has also met the same fate.'

'Then why' asked the man, 'do you dwell in so dreadful a place?'

'Because here there is no oppressive ruler,' she replied.

'Scholars', he said to his disciples, 'remember this. Oppressive rule is more cruel than a tiger.'

This man was Kung-fu-tze, Latinised as Confucius by the western scholars who were unable to pronounce his name.

Confucius had supreme confidence in his ability to re-order society. He was distressed to find that China was becoming weak. Lawlessness, corruption, and distress were on the increase. The crying need of the hour was a set of values which would serve as guidelines for the people around which they could rebuild their lives. It was to this task and to remedy such evil that Confucius applied himself.

Confucius based his system around two virtues—duty and love. A society could be secured only if each individual performed his social obligations.

In each relationship, a set of proprieties were to be observed, conventions established by Nature to be followed, and both these hallowed by history.

Duty alone was not sufficient. In addition, there had to be affection, charity, courage, loyalty, and good conduct.

Confucius was essentially a humanist. He insisted that Supreme blessedness was to be found here on earth, not in heaven, amongst men and not in the shadows.

The Ancient Chinese Religions

Clearly, Confucianism and Taoism were not religions as such. In fact, both developed separately and distinctly, more as forms of thought rather than as matters of faith. Taoism is a mystical philosophy that was founded in the sixth century BCE by Lao-tzu. He believed that behind and beyond all existence lay an infinite and impersonal essence called *Tao*. This was the Ultimate Happiness, and to gain this reality, man must forget the world and shun society, and return to nature or primeval life.

On the other hand, Confucius, much younger than Lao-tzu, was neither a religious leader nor a politician. He was a very wise and practical philosopher who taught tolerance to men and how to live happily in harmony with one another. He did not attempt to reform the existing religion, but organised the one which had existed in China from time immemorial.

What kind of religion did the ancient Chinese have?

It is possible to suggest that the ancient Chinese lived in a world which they believed was full of spirits and supernatural powers, and which had to be appeased by sacrifices and offerings. Both Taoism and Confucianism originated as rational thinking which avoided the strange and dark mysteries of religion, and instead, presented a simple code of conduct for people to practice.

Confucius is regarded as the First Teacher who gave his people the highest principles of moral and ethical conduct.

Confucius was born on 24 September and lived between 550 and 478 BCE.

He started his career as a teacher, using his home as his base. This was his vocation; he taught history, poetry, and the rules of decorum. His reputation and practical wisdom spread rapidly, and soon he had ardent disciples, who eagerly flocked to him. He required his students to display eagerness and alertness of mind, and was an exacting master. His students are recorded as saying that their Master was free from four things: 'He had no foregone conclusions, no arbitrary decisions, no obstinacy, and no egoism.'

He held several high official appointments, the highest of which was chief justice of his state. At the age of fifty, he was appointed as governor for five years.

He gave the next thirteen years of his life to the 'long trek' when he wandered from state to state proffering his unsought advice to rulers on how to improve their governments, and gave counsels of peace. He never got a chance to put his ideas into practice. His advice was rejected and the years slipped by. He carried himself with dignity and his humorous outlook towards life made him withstand the mockery of his failure.

He finally decided to give up his crusade to create order, and reform the moral and religious life of the people. Later, he returned to his own state of Li to a quiet, private life and devoted the rest of his days serenely by teaching and editing 'The Classics', and also indulging in a little writing himself. In 479 BC, at the age of 73, he died.

Classic of Filial Piety or *Hsia King* is his prime scripture. It bases the entire concept of religion on respect for parents, and worship of ancestors. The rulers of China were quick to realise that such a worship fostered conservatism, submissiveness, and a stable order, and declared it the most sacred book. Its influence has continued to dominate Chinese life and thought almost to the present day.

His Life: A Summation

Even though he might have been a failure as a politician and reformer, Confucius was no doubt one of the world's greatest teachers. His view of his life and achievements was that he had not been a success. He is recorded as saying. 'Alas, there is no one who knows me.'

The irony of fate is that though he was not acclaimed much or appreciated in his lifetime, his ability to win loyal friendships and disciples soon resulted in his becoming the 'founder' of Confucianism.

He repeatedly said that he was the transmitter and not the creator. This does not mean that he did not have creative capacity. Indeed, he was a genius. His simple belief was that harmony of conduct and morality is handed down from generation to generation and should be the foundation through which people regulate their conduct.

He possessed a deep knowledge of his country's history and literature. His dream was to create a state where the rulers and the ruled could live together with tolerance, harmony, and peace. He did not talk of spirituality.

The Master Teacher

Confucius was a teacher of morals, and it would be an error to classify his doctrines as religion. He recognised the existence of a Superior Being. It is interesting to note that beyond mere acknowledgement of the presence of God, Confucius did not elaborate on the nature of God.

A painting showing Confucius lecturing his disciples.

Therefore, he had very little to say about a Godhead. At the time he lived and wrote, people made offerings, sacrifices, lit candles, and spread incense to the spirits of their ancestors and others. Confucius did not venture to correct such ritualistic practices which he felt were best left to the private domain of an individual. He was more concerned with the development of the mind and its application to practical living.

Power and wealth could have been his for the asking if he had compromised with those in power. But, he preferred his integrity, and never regretted the choices that he had made.

After Confucius
His glorification began with his death. Soon, he was regarded as 'the mentor and model of ten thousand generations' in China.

A great deal of attention was given to his ideas and sayings. For almost two thousand years, every scholar has pored over his sayings for hours. Even the illiterate use his simple homely proverbs and anecdotes. It is a mystery of history that how a collection of sayings which are so unexciting and common place, could contribute or be the foundation of an entire civilisation. So much so, that Confucius is not only a part of the Chinese mind but is also undoubtedly one of the world's greatest teachers.

For over two thousand years, his teachings have greatly influenced a fifth of the world's population.

In the twentieth century, his birthday was declared as a national holiday in China. Confucius was a serene philosopher of great superiority and today, his sayings and compositions are the backbone of Chinese culture. The Chinese Government too, has been influenced by Confucius, and government officials are expected to have a knowledge of the Confucian Classics which teach an incorruptible code of political morality.

However, unlike the other religions of the world, Confucianism did not spread beyond the frontiers of China.

Confucius took the ancient theories of ancestor worship and gently brought around the emphasis from heaven to earth. He did not interfere with the conservative practices of the people that related to the worship of the dead, but stressed that it was more important to strengthen the ties of living families. He emphasised that the duties of the present members of the family towards one another were more important than their duties to the departed.

Activity Time

1) Confucius based his system around two virtues. What were they? Do you agree?
2) Would you regard Confucianism as a religion?
3) Although, he was 'no doubt one of the world's greatest teachers,' he was not appreciated in his lifetime. Why do you think this happened, as has happened with some other great men too?
4) How do the Chinese regard Confucius today?
5) Do you think Confucius' teachings can be followed even today?
6) What do you find the most interesting in Confucianism?

ZOROASTRIANISM

ROOTS

Introduction

A man dressed in white robes, with a flowing beard, stands before an assembly of royal courtiers and princelings. Before him, on a wooden platform, lies a magnificent horse on its side with its legs doubled. It cannot move. Only the whites of his rolling eyes show the extreme agony and pain that the animal is suffering. 'Can you cure him?' The king asks in a voice laden with anxiety.

The tall man looks at the king and says, 'Open your mind, and let in enlightenment.' The king is bewildered. The tall man continues, 'O King, I am truly the messenger of the Supreme God'. The king replies: 'I do believe you are Ahura Mazda's messenger.' To the amazement and joy of the onlookers, as soon as he stops speaking, one of the legs of the horse becomes free.

Twice more, in a ringing voice, the tall man makes the Queen and the Crown Prince repeat their belief and faith in Lord Ahura Mazda. The third leg of the horse now becomes free.

Finally, pointing to the jailer, the Man asks the King to question him about the alleged crime of Black Magic, for which he has been imprisoned. The keeper admits his complicity in the conspiracy to ruin the reputation of the Man. The King orders the banishment of all the wicked priests. Now, the horse stands on all four legs, in all its former glory. Then, raising his arms above his head, the Man proclaims, 'O Ahura Mazda, accept your follower, Kai Vishtaspa.' This man was Zarathustra.

His arrival had been foretold long before he was born. Supernatural portents were seen at the moment of his birth. His mother's home was illuminated by divine light, and the hearts of all evil beings were filled with fear and despair. Nobody knows for sure when he was born.

He lived in the steppe lands among nomads, who were crude and barbaric. He preached at a time when reading and writing were unknown among his people, so most of what he said was passed by word of mouth. Some historians place his birth around the sixth century BCE, but others put him in the reign of Kai Vishtaspa, in the tenth century.

Birth

His father was Pourashashpa and his mother, Dugdhova. He laughed when he was born, whereas other children cry at birth. Perhaps, this was to indicate to the world that misery is a sin and joy, an essential part of holiness. That is how his parents knew that he was blessed with Divine Grace, and had come to save this world from evil. His parents named him Zarathustra Spitama (He of the golden light).

Zarathustra's birth and the divine omens accompanying the birth, struck terror in the heart of the chieftain of an evil band in that area. He stole the baby and tried different means to kill him. He put him in the path of stampeding cattle, while at another time, he put the baby into a wolves' den, yet no harm came to him. Even when the baby was thrown into fire, the flames died down and turned into a bed of roses. Then the evil chieftain tried to stab the child to death, but his hand became paralysed, and the dagger fell from his lifeless hand.

According to the prevailing custom, when Zarathustra was fifteen, he was invested with the sacred *Kusti*. He now started taking active part in the religious activities of the community, and learned all about the mysteries of the faith. He felt an urge for deeper meditation and spiritual exercises, so, without a word or warning to anyone, he retired to the mighty Elbruz Mountains, to live in solitude to pray and contemplate. Here, he called on the True and Only God Ahura Mazda for guidance.

Learning

It is believed that between the age of thirty and forty, he felt himself in the presence of Ahura Mazda (the God of Zarathustra) and attained illumination. During these divine visitations, he experienced a call that asked him to spread and preach whatever he had learned from Ahura Mazda. However, he had to go through many trials and temptations caused by the 'evil spirit', but he remained unswerving in his faith in Ahura Mazda, the Lord of Light.

He won his struggles against the evil spirit, Satan, who offered him the entire world, great riches, and treasures, if only he would renounce his Lord. Satan even threatened to kill him. Ahura Mazda then appeared to him and gave into his keeping the *Avesta* or the 'Book of Knowledge and Wisdom', and directed him to spread its Word to the world.

Trials and Temptations

As it happens to most reformers or prophets, at first, Zarathustra was ridiculed and persecuted. He had to go through a lot of troubles, temptations, and struggles against a society that was riddled with evil and corruption. He fought to establish the Kingdom of God and Truth in the world, and worked and preached for the moral welfare of mankind. He taught in a simple language that doing good to one's fellowmen is the true way to happiness and self-perfection. He stated that the object of religion or of state or of society is the cultivation of morality and compassion.

Preaching

When Zarathustra appeared, the religion of the Irano-Aryans was polytheistic nature-worship. He was pained to find people worshipping their ancestors, animals, and the elements of Nature like the earth, air, and sun. He revolted against this practice and declared that there was only one God, Ahura Mazda. He proclaimed and preached that the other gods were manifestations of the divine attributes of Ahura Mazda.

Kai Vishtaspa, himself, helped spread this new faith and fought several wars in defence of the new religion, till the Zoroastrian faith became firmly established.

People from far and near heard of Zarathustra's fame and flocked to the Court of Kai Vishtaspa to hear the Holy Prophet speak of this great new religion. Zarathustra emphasised over and over again that he was only a Prophet, and was teaching the Holy Truths that had been revealed to him.

These Holy Truths included:

Honour your God daily

Be a good father, a good neighbour, and a good master

There was great rejoicing in the land at this simple message and people toiled hard on their farms and in various other occupations. They produced more, and wealth and happiness increased.

The End

The end for Zarathustra was near at hand when he was seventy-seven years old. He felt that his appointed task was almost complete.

He sat at the Fire Temple lost in meditation. Outside, the kingdom's enemies and hostile priests had launched an attack, mercilessly slaughtering the inhabitants. They had only one aim—and that was to kill Zarathustra, and destroy his faith. Suddenly, an assassin dashed into the Temple, and stabbed the kneeling Prophet to death. As his life ebbed away, Zarathustra murmured 'O Mazda, the only One, *Ashem Vohu*' and Zarathustra threw off his worldly bonds and the great soul now free, merged into eternity.

Shoots
Spread of Zoroastrian Faith

Kai Vishtaspa was the first King of Iran who adopted and established the Zoroastrian religion in his kingdom.
The concept of Zoroastrian religion was:
Righteousness in thought, word, and deed.

Righteousness is the supreme code of universal conduct; righteousness for the sake of righteousness only, and not for the sake of material gain, was a very liberal theory.

The Landing–Parsis landing on the shores of India are now amongst the 'elite' of India's population.

King Jadhav Rana granting permission to the Parsis to stay in India.

The progress of this religion was not very dramatic, and it mainly flourished among the Iranian people. For some time, the records are also not clear.

At the end of sixth century AD, came the new powerful religion of the Muslims. The Muslims invaded Iran and in 652 AD, the last Zoroastrian king died. The Zoroastrians date their calendar from his coronation in 632 AD and use the convention AY.

The military victory of the Arab armies saw the persecution of Zoroastrians. Their property was confiscated and extra tax was imposed on non-muslims. At times, they were also killed if they did not convert to Islam. The brave and devout Zoroastrians went into hiding in villages rather than be converted to Islam and their numbers seriously declined. Life had become extremely difficult for them. Seeking a new land where they could practice their religion in freedom, they crossed the ocean and travelled to India and called themselves Parsis that is the 'Persians.'

This brave band of devout, harassed, and hunted men and women who had suffered untold miseries for their religion, were caught in a storm and their small boats were in danger of drowning. The priests prayed to God for help, and vowed that if they reached land safely, they would build a temple for their God in thanksgiving. It seemed as if suddenly there was divine intervention, their God Ahura Mazda helped them and they landed in Div on the South coast of Kathiawar. From there, they sailed to Sanjan.

This event took place around 936 AD. The ruler gave them permission to settle on his land. He imposed certain conditions which would ensure that the Parsis did not disturb the Indian way of life.

These conditions were:
1) The adoption of Gujarati as their mother tongue
2) The adoption of the local dress, and local marriage customs
3) The surrender of all weapons

Their priests accepted all these conditions, and then gave the *Raja* an idea of their religion in sixteen Sanskrit shlokas. It showed how the Parsis were ready to honour the Hindu religion and customs, and manifested their eagerness to assimilate and integrate into the Hindu State.

The Raja issued a proclamation inviting all citizens to assemble in an open meadow, where he took his seat, dressed in royal robes, and fabulous jewellery. He had with him, his mounted bodyguards, dressed in white, holding their glittering spears.

At a signal from him, the Persian refugees were presented to him. Their frail old priest, holding the sacred fire, was the spokesman. He spoke through an interpreter.

'What is it you want from us, O strangers from a far land?' asked Jadhav Rana, the king.

'Freedom of worship, Sir,' replied the old priest.

'Granted. What else do you wish?'

'Freedom to bring up our young in our own traditions and customs.'

'Granted. What else do you wish?'

'A small piece of land that we could cultivate so that we may not be a burden to the people among whom we live.'

'Granted. In return what will you do for the country of your adoption?' the king asked.

The old priest asked for a bowl to be filled with milk, and some sugar to be stirred in the bowl.

Holding it up in his trembling hands, he asked:
'Does any man see the sugar in the bowl of milk?'
All shook their heads, and the Parsis were accepted by the Indians as one of their own.

The new arrivals kept their promise to Ahura Mazda, to build a Fire Temple for their deliverance and safe landing. The fire consecrated after their arrival has been burning in the Temple at Udvada, and it is the most important centre of pilgrimage for the Parsis.

That day onwards, this small enlightened community has never asked for any privileges or protection, but has been enterprising and helpful to their mother country, of which they are a proud part.

It is very curious that the Parsis are very few in number. In India, they are within a hundred thousand, and about fifteen thousand in Iran.

The Navjote

This is the most important ceremony for the Parsis; it is like Baptism for the Christians. Traditionally, it takes place about the age of puberty and the same rites and rules apply for boys as well as girls.

The ceremony of investing the child with the sacred shirt *Sudre*, and the sacred thread, *Kusti* is known as *Navjote*. The ritual Fire, the symbol of righteousness, burns nearby. On a tray, a new sudre and kusti, with a new set of clothes are kept.

During the ceremony, almost the same auspicious Indian articles like flowers, rice, kumkum, betel leaf, and coconut are used, and the child is blessed by all those who are present.

The ritual: A Sudre (the garment of the Good Mind, this

sacred shirt is made of white muslin) and Kusti (a narrow band woven from sheep's wool which is wound thrice around the waist) is the first public declaration of belonging to the Zoroastrian religion.

A Parsi is born a Parsi; he can never be converted to be a Parsi. By putting on 'the armour of the religion', the child chooses of its own free will to fight for his God. Navjote is the initiation into spiritual responsibility.

Navroz: It is the Parsi New Year which celebrates the renewal of life in spring. The festival is also a means of emphasising the Zoroastrian joy in worship, the brotherhood of man, and the (spiritual duty) love of generosity.

Fire and Fire Temples

Fire was a natural religious symbol. To this, Zarathustra added the idea that 'it is a symbol of righteousness, and likewise it should illuminate our hearts and purify our lives. We are worshippers of the One Pure God, and the Fire is a symbol of His purity and strength.'

The nomads did not stay long enough at one place to build temples or statues. The cooking fire was the focus of their religious activities. This developed into the Temple cult of Fire. They considered Fire to be the living, visible aspect of the Divine. The Fire temples became an important and popular part of religion, and many such temples were built by successive rulers.

Parsi Marriage

The true Zoroastrian marriage is the sacred union of two souls who complement each other in the ideal practice of doing good and maintaining self-denial, which should be the keynote of life.

It is interesting that even though the Parsis do not know Sanskrit, many of their mantras are recited in Sanskrit.

The Tower of Silence: Death

The Parsis have different rites associated with death, than most other faiths. The Zoroastrians believe that death is a weapon of the devil and the aim of funeral rites is to restrict evil and keep it away from good healthy living creation.

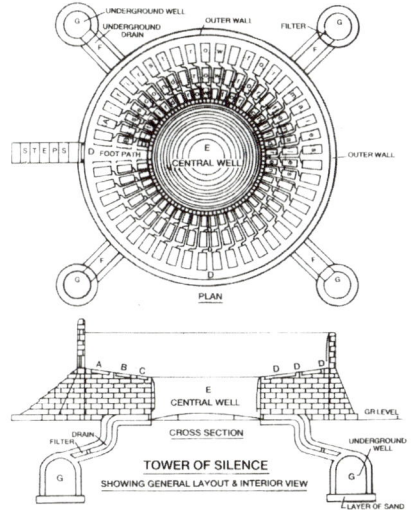

The dead body is neither burnt nor buried, but is kept on a high tower, and exposed to the elements of nature where the vultures and the carrion birds dispose it. The idea is that a dead body must be disposed as soon as possible without polluting the elements, as even burning would defile the pure flame. The body is washed and wrapped in clean but old clothes (to avoid waste). It is placed in a *'dakhma'* or a 'Tower of Silence'.

This tower is a circular stone tower, with high protective walls, but open to the sky, so that the birds of prey have easy access.

The dead are remembered in annual ceremonies, with a spirit of reverence and in the belief that their spiritual presence is with the living, and will help them.

The oldest Zoroastrian scripture known is the Avesta; it

consists of *Gathas* which are the composition of Zarathustra.

The Gathas reflect the personality of the Prophet Zarathustra and are the direct dialogues between God and the Prophet. They were first destroyed in Persepolis by the invading armies of Alexandra, and later, by the Arabs.

The conflict between good and evil spirits dominates Zarathustra's entire teaching. It is also clear that Ahura Mazda, the Supreme God, stands above and beyond them, always on the side of good.

The Concept of Religion

Zarathustra did not claim to be a metaphysician or a philosopher. He stressed that he was a Prophet, who had divine revelation from the True God, Ahura Mazda, and it is a revealed religion of faith and devotion. Ahura Mazda is all-pervading, omniscient, changeless, benevolent, merciful, the holiest, and perfect.

Zarathustra was the first Prophet to propound the dual theory of God and Satan. He realised from his experience of disharmony and vice, that dishonesty, crime, and evil also prevailed in the world; that besides the good God, there was an evil spirit like Satan. These two powers are symbolised as the genii of light and darkness, respectively. The evil spirit is the negation of all that is good, honest, and pure in the mind and body.

It is further said: 'Man is free in his choice, he can select the good or the bad; hence, he is responsible for his actions.'

By presenting this picture of a world in conflict between the good and the bad to the people, he encouraged them to strive for perfection, and to shun evil.

He placed before them another new concept of God as a punisher of Evil, and rewarder of Good. Finally, he made a clear reference to the immortality of the soul, and life here-after in his two famous words *'Frasho Kereti'*, meaning 'make life lasting.'

Man's Destiny

Zoroastrians believe that when a man dies, his soul goes for its Judgement. Its good thoughts, words, and deeds are weighed in balance against its evil thoughts, words, and deeds.

The good soul is rewarded, and the evil soul is punished. 'It is all in the soul', said Zarathustra, 'Our Hell and Heaven.'

His Teachings were the three Eternal Truths:
Good thoughts
Good words
Good deeds

The term that his followers use to describe Zoroastrianism is, 'The Good Religion.' It has no doctrine of original sin, or one man dying to save all. Every man is responsible for his own destiny. Extremes of enjoyment or asceticism—one or the other, is wrong. The right path is one of moderation, which holds the body and soul in balance.

Another joyful belief of Zoroastrianism is that because God is wholly good, the world which He created is also good. God's nature is to expand and be creative, whereas, the devil is the opposite and is destructive.

Zarathustra did not believe that ecstasy or happiness could be achieved by practising the virtues of a hermit or a recluse who flees from the temptations of the world, and seeks salvation for himself.

Activity Time

1) Where would you find Zoroastrians today?
2) In 936 AD, when a group of them came to India, they made certain promises to the Ruler of Gujarat. How did that make you feel?
3) Do you think it is fair to demand rights and privileges based on your own religion in your host country?
4) What do you know about the Tower of Silence? Compare that to man's selfishness and complete disregard for other beings, Nature, and the Elements.
5) Is religion only about respect to God? Or, is it about respect to other human beings and other creatures too. If yes, why?
6) Why do you think Fire is worshipped by the Parsis and other religions?
7) Why was Zoroastrianism called 'the Good Religion' by its followers?
8) What do you find the most interesting in Zoroastrianism?

THE BAHA'I FAITH

ROOTS

Introduction
The Baha'i Faith is the youngest of the world's independent religions. It sees itself as a revealed religion, which has been offered by God for the betterment of the human race.

The religion developed from the teachings of two visionaries in the nineteenth century in Iran.

Bab: Gate of God
The first one was Siyyid Ali Muhammad (1819-50) who was called the *Bab* (meaning 'the Gate'). He was a descendant of Prophet Mohammed through both his parents. His mission was to establish an independent religion and to prepare the way for the coming of 'Him whom God shall make Manifest', the expected Messenger of God of the previous religious scriptures.

This simple message was enthusiastically received in Iran by people from all walks of life, rich and poor, ignorant and learned—all wanted to know more about this religion. As the message of his teachings of love and kindness to the poor spread through the country, the rulers of Iran were alarmed, and they started persecuting the followers of Bab. He was finally executed with a disciple in 1850.

Bab was the forerunner of a greater Messenger than himself and that was Baha'u'llah. Bab brought new laws which concerned prayers, fasting, marriage, divorce, and inheritance.

Baha'u'llah: The Glory of God

The son of a minister at the court of the Shah of Iran, Baha'u'llah was born into a rich and noble family. All comforts of life were his for the asking, and he was brought up in the lap of luxury. He was instructed in the main teachings of Islam, literature, and poetry, and was taught calligraphy.

He was a brilliant child and at the tender age of seven, he astonished everyone by winning a property dispute in the court of the Shah. When very young, he married a girl from a wealthy family, but both partners shared the same simple tastes. They helped the needy and poor and came to be known as the 'Father and Mother of the poor'.

In the summer of 1844, after reading a scroll of the Bab's writings, Baha'u'llah gave his full support to this movement, which urged the reduction of the disparity between the rich and the poor. At that time, he was only twenty-seven. But from then onwards, his life was one round of captivity, persecution, and exile from one country to another.

Whilst in prison, Baha'u'llah had a mystical experience which revealed to him that he was 'the One whom God shall make manifest', and whose coming had been foretold by the Bab.

Stripped of his wealth and possessions, Baha'u'llah was exiled from Iran, and stayed ten years in Iraq, spreading the teachings of Bab. He wrote several books, and had a large number of followers, who were respected for their purity and integrity and who set a high standard of conduct for all to follow.

Before being banished to Constantinople, Baha'u'llah made a formal declaration to his followers that he was indeed the Promised One who was awaited by all.

The Iranian officials who were jealous of his popularity, forced him to again be banished to Adrianopole. From here, he wrote about his mission to the monarchs of Europe and called on them to recognise his Faith. He described the aim of the new Faith as one to usher in a new world order and world peace.

Again, the Iranians caused him to be imprisoned in Akka in Palestine, and perpetual banishment was imposed on Baha'u'llah. However, his influence spread, and people flocked to listen to him, and loved him for his goodness and wisdom.

He passed away in May 1892 and was mourned by thousands of his followers.

Shoots

'Abdu'l-Baha, the eldest son of Baha'u'llah was born in 1844. He learned all he knew from his father, and accompanied him in his exile. Baha'u'llah appointed him his heir and head of the Baha'i Faith and its interpreter. In 1911, he travelled to England to give lectures and then to Europe and America, where he spoke of his father's mission. Many people accepted these new teachings. Abdu'l-Baha said in London, 'The gift of God to this enlightened age is the knowledge of oneness of mankind and the fundamental oneness of religion.'

A group of Baha'is belonging to different nationalities

Now, this Faith has centres in over 343 countries, islands, and territories. Although it originated in Iran, a Muslim country, it is the youngest religion to have spread to all corners of the world within just 150 years.

Baha'u'llah wrote a number of spiritual and mystical books to guide the faithful. His main theme was oneness of humanity, and unity even in diversity.

Baha'is believe that each age has their own special needs and special problems. Thus, there was a special Messenger of God like Krishna, Zoroaster, Moses, Buddha, Jesus, Mohammed, and Baha'u'llah, to fulfil the specific needs of that particular period. Each one founded a religion which was followed by and inspired millions of humans and drew them nearer to God.

The Baha'is revere the various Manifestations of God, and regard the scriptures of all the world's religions as sacred. The Baha'is believe in religion being progressive, hence different prophets came from time to time to guide humanity and change the religious laws to suit that particular age.

Baha'is accept Baha'u'llah as the latest of God's Manifestations to appear on Earth. By doing away with prejudice of religion, race, class, and colour, he brought unity among the religions of the world, and thereby, world unity.

Rules for Good Living

Behaviour: Man should try to be honest, loving, generous, and forgiving. He should be detached, and not be affected by adversity or be elated by riches.

Prayer and Fasting: These are necessary as they renew a man spiritually and physically.

Service to Humanity: The daily work should be regarded as worship of God.

Teaching the Faith: There are no priests or ministers in this Faith. They believe that each man should be a giver of the Baha'i message to others, must have firm faith in God, and live up to the high standards of Baha'i teachings.

Abstinence from Drugs and Alcohol.

Obedience to Governments: A Baha'i must abide by the laws of the land in which he lives, and seek peaceful solutions to problems.

Patriotism of a new kind (Baha'u'llah): 'It is not for him to pride himself who loveth his own country but rather for him who loveth the whole world.'

'The Earth is but one country, and mankind its citizens.'

Activity Time

1) Which is the youngest of the World's independent religions? It professes to unite all religions. Do you agree?
2) It also professes to teach a new kind of patriotism. What is that? Do you agree with it?
3) The believers of the Baha'i faith believe in the oneness of all religions. What are their beliefs? Would you like to live in such a world which is not divided by caste, creed, faith, and colour? Give your reasons, either way.
4) What do you find the most interesting in the Baha'i faith?

Ponder over what you have read, then answer the following four questions:

1. Is any one religion the true religion and the only path to God, Moksha, Nirvana, Heaven, Jannat? Are all religions true?

2. Do you think that God revealed Himself/Herself to only the Prophet or Founder of any one particular religion or faith?

3. After having learned about 10 World Religions, do you see any fundamental unity in all of them?

4. Should one respect all religions, faiths and beliefs or should one be fanatical about one's own beliefs and expect others to follow suit?